Microsoft®

Outlook® 2010 Plain & Simple

Jim Boyce

Published with the authorization of Microsoft Corporation by:
O'Reilly Media, Inc.
1005 Gravenstein Highway North
Sebastopol, California 95472

Printed and bound in the United States of America.

ISBN: 978-0-7356-2734-5

3 4 5 6 7 8 9 10 11 QGT 7 6 5 4 3 2

Microsoft Press titles may be purchased for educational, business or sales promotional use. Online editions are also available for most titles (*http://my.safaribooksonline.com*). For more information, contact our corporate/institutional sales department: (800) 998-9938 or *corporate@ oreilly.com*. Visit our website at *microsoftpress.oreilly.com*. Send comments to *mspinput@microsoft.com*.

Microsoft, Microsoft Press, ActiveX, Excel, FrontPage, Internet Explorer, PowerPoint, SharePoint, Webdings, Windows, and Windows 7 are either registered trademarks or trademarks of Microsoft Corporation in the United States and/or other countries. Other product and company names mentioned herein may be the trademarks of their respective owners.

Unless otherwise noted, the example companies, organizations, products, domain names, e-mail addresses, logos, people, places, and events depicted herein are fictitious, and no association with any real company, organization, product, domain name, e-mail address, logo, person, place, or event is intended or should be inferred.

This book expresses the author's views and opinions. The information contained in this book is provided without any express, statutory, or implied warranties. Neither the author, O'Reilly Media, Inc., Microsoft Corporation, nor their respective resellers or distributors, will be held liable for any damages caused or alleged to be caused either directly or indirectly by such information.

Acquisitions and Developmental Editor: Kenyon Brown
Production Editor: Rachel Monaghan
Editorial Production: Online Training Solutions, Inc.
Technical Reviewer: Vincent Averello
Indexer: Potomac Indexing, LLC
Compositor: Ron Bilodeau
Illustrator: Robert Romano

[2012-10-12]

Contents

7 Working with Contacts 99

8 Managing a Calendar 125

What do you think of this book? We want to hear from you!

Microsoft is interested in hearing your feedback so we can continually improve our books and learning resources for you. To participate in a brief online survey, please visit:

www.microsoft.com/learning/booksurvey/

Acknowledgments

I've authored and coauthored over 50 books, and each one has been a unique project. Each one has also been a group effort. I'd like to thank everyone at Microsoft and O'Reilly that helped get this project off the ground and for guiding it to completion. Thanks also go to Carole McClendon with Waterside Productions for her help in developing the opportunity. Special thanks also to Ken Brown for his help in launching the project.

A very big thanks to Vince Averello for an outstanding job of tech-editing the book for accuracy—an extremely important task for any good book. Thanks to Microsoft and O'Reilly for creating an awesome design. I also extend thanks to the rest of the editorial and production team for all of their efforts in turning out a great book. They are: Kathleen Atkins; Jaime Odell and Jean Trenery with Online Training Solutions, Inc.; Seth Maislin with Potomac Indexing, Inc.; and Ron Bilodeau, Rachel Monaghan, and Rob Romano at O'Reilly.

Finally, I offer my deep appreciation to my wife, Julie, who put up with me revising not one, but two, Outlook 2010 books while also holding down a full-time job.

Introduction: About This Book

I f you want to get the most from your computer and your software with the least amount of time and effort—and who doesn't?—this book is for you. You'll find *Microsoft® Outlook® 2010 Plain & Simple* to be a straightforward, easy-to-read reference tool. With the premise that your computer should work for you, not you for it, this book's purpose is to help you get your work done quickly and efficiently so that you can get away from the computer and live your life.

No Computerspeak!

Let's face it—when there's a task you don't know how to do but need to get done in a hurry, or when you're stuck in the middle of a task and can't figure out what to do next, there's nothing more frustrating than having to read page after page of technical background material. You want the information you need—nothing more, nothing less—and you want it now! It should be easy to find and understand.

That's what this book is all about. It's written in plain English—no jargon. There's no single task in the book that takes more than a couple pages. Just look the task up in the index or the table of contents, turn to the page, and there's the information you need, laid out in an illustrated step-by-step format. You don't get bogged down by the whys and wherefores: just follow the steps and get your work done.

Occasionally, you might want to turn to another page if the procedure you're working on is accompanied by a "See Also." That's because a lot of tasks overlap, and I didn't want to keep repeating myself. I've scattered some useful Tips here and there, and thrown in a "Try This" or a "Caution" once in a while, but I tried to remain true to the heart and soul of a Plain & Simple book, which is that the information you need should be available to you at a glance.

Useful Tasks

I've packed this book with procedures for everything I could think of that you might want to do, from the simplest tasks to some of the more esoteric ones, whether you use Outlook at home or on the road.

And the Easiest Way to Do Them

In this book, I want to document the easiest way to accomplish a task. Outlook often provides a multitude of methods to accomplish a single result—which can be daunting or delightful, depending on the way you like to work. If you tend to stick with one favorite and familiar approach, I think the methods described in this book are the way to go. If you like trying out alternative techniques, go ahead! Outlook invites exploration, and you're likely to discover ways of doing things that you think are easier or that you like better than mine. If you do, that's great! It's exactly what the developers of Outlook had in mind when they provided so many alternatives.

A Quick Overview

Your computer probably came with Outlook preinstalled, but if you have to install it yourself, the Setup Wizard makes installation so simple that you won't need my help anyway. So, unlike many computer books, this one doesn't start with installation instructions and a list of system requirements.

Next, you don't have to read the sections of this book in any particular order. You can jump in, get the information you need, and then close the book and keep it near your computer until the next time you need to know how to get something done. But that doesn't mean the information is scattered wildly about. The book is organized so that the tasks you want to accomplish are arranged in two levels—you'll find the overall type of task you're looking for under a main section title such as "Working with Contact Groups," "Setting Up E-Mail Accounts," "Communicating with Contacts," and so on. Then, in each of those sections, smaller tasks are arranged in a loose progression from the simplest to the more complex.

Section 2 provides an overview of the most common changes and notable new features in Outlook 2010, such as the ribbon. If you have been a user of Outlook 2007 or earlier, Section 2 gives you a good idea of what's new.

Section 3 introduces you to Outlook functions; it explains how to start and exit the program, work with the Outlook program window, and use the standard set of folders in Outlook. You also learn how to set up e-mail accounts, import data into Outlook from other programs, and work with items such as e-mail messages, contacts, and appointments. Information about how to get help and troubleshoot problems rounds out the section.

Sections 4 and 5 explain how to work with e-mail messages in Outlook, including addressing messages, using Address Book, and working with contact groups. Section 4 teaches you how to change and format message text to add emphasis or highlight information. You also learn how to incorporate designs and color schemes to give messages the look of stationery. Section 4 finishes with a look at how to send files with messages, review messages you've already sent, and keep messages in the Drafts folder until you're ready to send them. Section 5 covers several topics about receiving and reading e-mail and helps you manage, filter, and follow up on messages.

In Section 6, you learn how to work with Really Simple Syndication (RSS) feeds in Outlook. Through RSS, you can subscribe to specific Web content, such as news, event listings, headlines, and other information, and you can receive and view that information right in Outlook—you don't need a separate tool for working with RSS.

Keeping track of your contacts' addresses, phone numbers, and other information is one of the main uses for Outlook, and Section 7 acquaints you with the Contacts folder. You learn how to add new contacts, view and change contacts, and find a particular person. The section also explains how to organize contacts, schedule meetings for a contact, and communicate with people through the Contacts folder. The section finishes with a look at how to share contacts with others, keep track of phone calls, and associate contacts with items such as tasks.

Section 8 covers the Calendar folder and how to view your schedule, add appointments and meetings, associate files or other items with schedule items, and work with reminders. You also learn how to share your calendar, print calendars, and use the To-Do Bar to keep track of your tasks without leaving the Calendar folder.

Section 9 expands on Section 8's coverage of tasks and explains how to use the Tasks folder. You can assign tasks to yourself or to others, associate contacts and other items with tasks, and mark tasks as complete.

Section 10 covers mobile features of Outlook 2010, such as setting up alerts to your mobile device for calendar events, messages, and voice mail. Section 10 also explains how to set up and use a text messaging service to send text messages from Outlook.

Section 11 explains how to integrate SharePoint sites with Outlook, which enables you to view shared calendars, contacts, document libraries, and other SharePoint items in Outlook. You can also work with those SharePoint items right from Outlook without ever opening the SharePoint site. Section 11 also looks at the presence features in Outlook that help you see when others are online, and communicate with them using collaboration tools like Office Communicator.

Section 12 helps you start to organize the data you keep in Outlook. Here you learn to create categories and organize Outlook items with categories, create and manage folders, delete items, and automatically move items out of your regular Outlook storage file and into an archive file. Archiving keeps your Outlook data file lean while still letting you hang on to important messages.

Section 13 helps you work with and manage the files in which Outlook stores your data. You learn to create new data files, import and export items in Outlook, and back up and restore your Outlook data file.

Outlook offers a wealth of options you can use to change the way the program looks and works, and Section 14 shows you how to set options for each of the Outlook folders and item types. The section also explains how to customize the Outlook Navigation Pane, ribbon, and Quick Access toolbar.

A Few Assumptions

I had to make a few educated guesses about you—my audience—when I started writing this book. Perhaps your computer is solely for personal use—e-mail, surfing the Internet, playing games, and so on. Possibly your work allows you to telecommute. Or maybe you run a small home-based business. Taking all these possibilities into account, I assumed that you either use a stand-alone home computer or that you have two or more computers connected so that you could share files, a printer, and so on. I also assumed that you have an Internet connection.

Another assumption is that—initially, anyway—you use Outlook just as it came, meaning that you use the standard views and standard menus rather than custom ones, and that you use your little friend the mouse in the traditional way: that is, you point and click to select an item and then double-click to open it. If you prefer using the mouse as if you are working on a Web page—pointing to an item to select it and then opening it with a single click—you can easily do so. To switch between single-click and double-click, open the Folder Options applet from the Control Panel. Use the Click Items As Follows controls to choose the method you prefer. However, because my working style is somewhat traditional, and because Outlook is set up to work in the traditional style, that's the style followed in the procedures and graphics throughout this book.

A Final Word (or Two)

I had three goals in writing this book:

- Whatever you want to do, I want the book to help you get it done.

- I want the book to help you discover how to do things you didn't know you wanted to do.

- And, finally, if I achieve the first two goals, I'm well on the way to the third: I want this book to help you enjoy using Outlook.

I hope you have as much fun using *Microsoft Outlook 2010 Plain & Simple* as I've had writing it. The best way to learn is by doing—jump right in!

2

What's New in Outlook 2010?

Microsoft Outlook 2010 includes lots of new features that improve usability and add functionality. Many of the familiar features in previous versions are improved, reworked, or fine-tuned in Outlook 2010. All of these changes combine to make Outlook 2010 a great tool for collaboration, communication, and time and information management.

A New Interface

Like the other Office applications, Outlook 2010 sports a new interface, but the differences in Outlook are more pronounced than the differences were in Outlook 2007 from its previous version. Outlook 2010 now fully implements the ribbon used by the other Office applications.

Use the Ribbon

Like most of the other Office 2010 applications, all of the Outlook windows use the ribbon to organize and expose commands and features. The main benefit of the ribbon is that it logically organizes features and makes the most commonly used ones easily discoverable.

1. Open Outlook and note the ribbon in the main Outlook window. Previous versions used a standard Windows-style menu bar and toolbars.

2. Click Inbox in the Navigation Pane to open the Inbox.

3. Click New E-mail to start a new message.

4. Click in the body of the message.

5. Click the Bold button in the Basic Text group of the Message tab.

6. Type some text.

7. Click the Options tab.

(continued on next page)

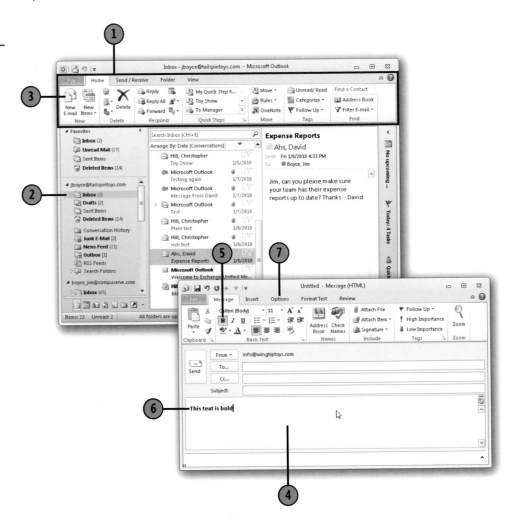

Use the Ribbon *(continued)*

8 Click Bcc to show the Bcc field.

9 Click Page Color and click on a color.

10 Click Close.

11 Click No when you're prompted to save changes.

Tip

Outlook 2010 incorporates several additional improvements that are not covered in detail in this book. To learn more, see *Microsoft Outlook 2010 Inside Out*, by Jim Boyce (Microsoft Press, 2010).

Tip

You find the Quick Access Toolbar above the ribbon next to the File tab. You can customize the Quick Access Toolbar to add the commands that you use most often so that they all are readily available.

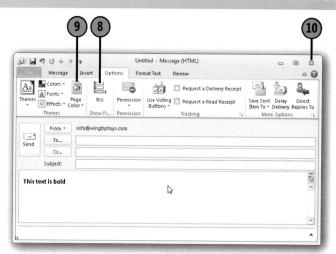

The Navigation Pane

The Navigation Pane gives you quick access to all of your Outlook folders (Inbox, Calendar, and so on) and changes depending on which folder you're using. For example, when you open the Calendar folder, the objects offered in the Navigation Pane reflect features available in the Calendar, such as views. When you select the Mail icon, all of your e-mail accounts appear in the Navigation Pane. In addition, SharePoint lists that are connected to Outlook also appear there, as does your Online Archive, if your Exchange Server mailbox is configured for one.

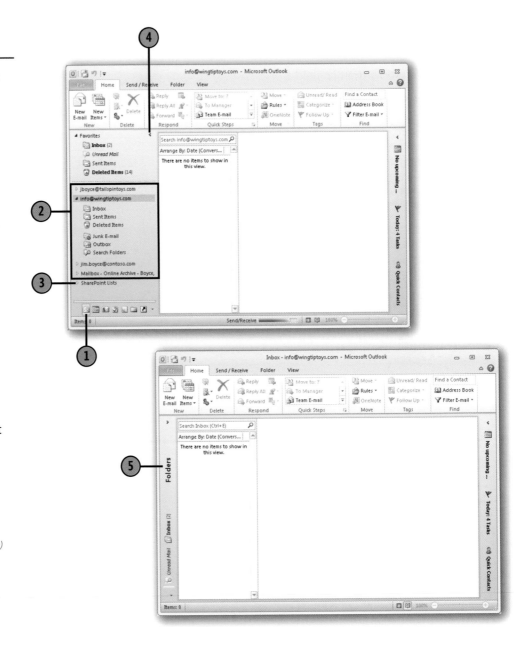

1. Click the Mail icon to open the Inbox.

2. Note the multiple e-mail accounts, which use each account's e-mail address as the name for that branch in the Navigation Pane.

3. Note the SharePoint Lists branch, which shows all connected SharePoint lists.

4. Click the Minimize the Navigation Pane button.

5. Click the Folders button to open an expanding Folder list.

(continued on next page)

The Navigation Pane *(continued)*

6 Click a folder to open it.

7 Click the Configure Buttons button.

8 Choose a folder to open.

9 Click the Expand the Navigation Pane button to restore the Navigation Pane.

Tip

When the Navigation Pane is minimized, you can expand it for temporary use by clicking the Folders button on the minimized Navigation Pane. When you click on something outside of the Navigation Pane (such as on a message), the Folders list minimizes again.

See Also

For information about the Navigation Pane, see "Exploring Outlook Folders" on page 33.

Backstage

The Office Backstage view is new in Outlook 2010 as it is in the other Office 2010 applications. It incorporates many of the commands found on the File menu in previous editions of Outlook, as well as commands from the former Tools menu. Backstage is where you go to save, print, set options, and perform other administrative tasks.

1. Click the File tab on the ribbon to open Backstage view.

2. Choose an account to view its settings and options.

3. Note the account-specific options in the Contents Pane.

4. Click Open.

5. Note the options for opening calendars, other Outlook .pst files, another user's folder, and import or export options.

6. Click Print.

(continued on next page)

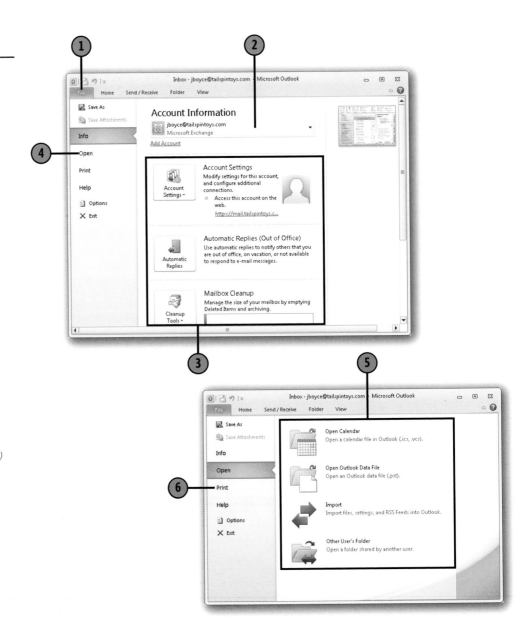

Backstage *(continued)*

(7) Click to choose a printer.

(8) Click to set print options.

(9) Choose what you want to print.

(10) Preview the results.

(11) Click to print the selected item.

(12) Click Home to return to the current folder.

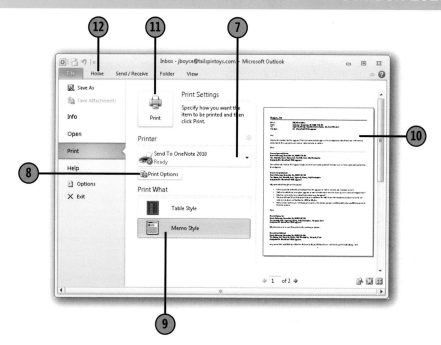

Views

With the introduction of the ribbon in Outlook 2010, the most commonly used commands are now located in the various tabs on the ribbon. Views are a good example. You can quickly access a particular view by choosing it from the Change View button on the ribbon, or you can change settings for the current view by clicking View Settings on the ribbon.

1. Click the Mail icon to open the Inbox.

2. Click the view tab on the ribbon.

3. Click Change View, and then choose a view.

4. Click Arrange By.

5. Choose a field to organize the view by that field.

6. Choose how you want to view the Navigation Pane, Reading Pane, and To-Do Bar.

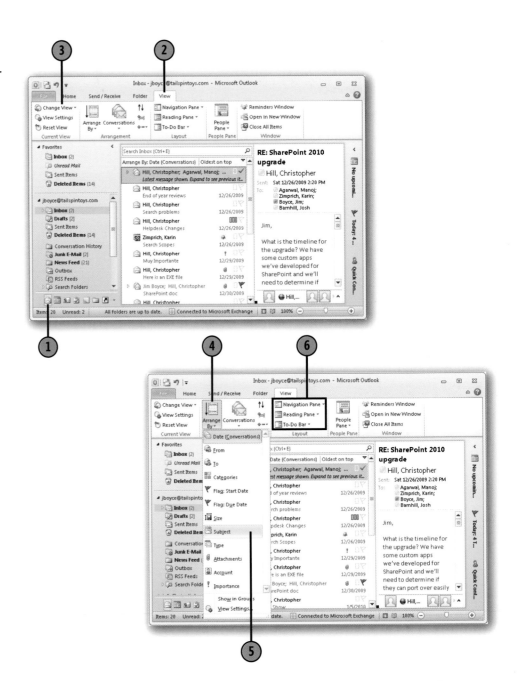

E-mail Changes

You'll find a handful of really great additions in Outlook 2010 for messaging in general and e-mail in particular. Conversation view is much improved, Quick Steps help you automate frequent tasks, and other new features for Microsoft Exchange Server 2010 users make Outlook 2010 even better as a mail client for Exchange Server.

Conversations and Quick Steps

The Conversation feature in Outlook 2010 organizes messages by Conversation thread: Outlook displays related messages together regardless of their location in your mail store. Quick Steps let you create multi-step actions to perform against messages, much like run-on-demand rules (rules you can run when you need them).

1. Click the Mail icon to open the Inbox.

2. Click to expand a message conversation.

3. Note that Outlook displays messages in a Conversation from multiple folders.

4. Outlook provides a visual indicator to show which message replies are related.

5. Click to set up a Quick Step that moves messages to a specific folder.

(continued on next page)

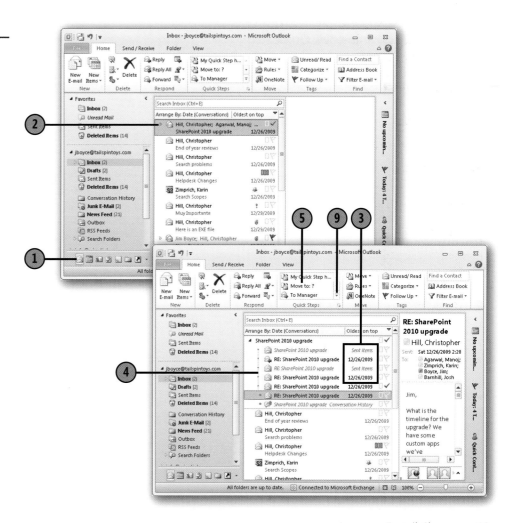

Conversations and Quick Steps (continued)

(6) Enter a name for the Quick Step.

(7) Choose a folder, or use the option Always Ask For Folder to have Outlook prompt you for a destination.

(8) Click Save to save the new Quick Step.

(9) Click to view other default Quick Steps.

(10) Click to Create a custom Quick Step.

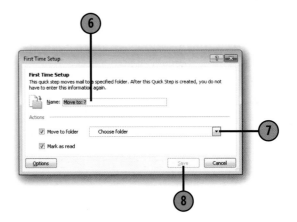

Exchange Server Additions

Outlook 2010 includes some new features for people with Exchange Server mailboxes who use Outlook 2010 to access those mailboxes. The MailTips feature warns you of hazards when you try to perform mail-related actions that might pose some risk, such as mailing a message to a very large number of users or to contact groups for which you don't have permission to send messages. You can also use multiple Exchange Server accounts in the same profile (even on different Exchange Server environments), and you can use the online archive feature in Exchange Server 2010 to archive messages automatically.

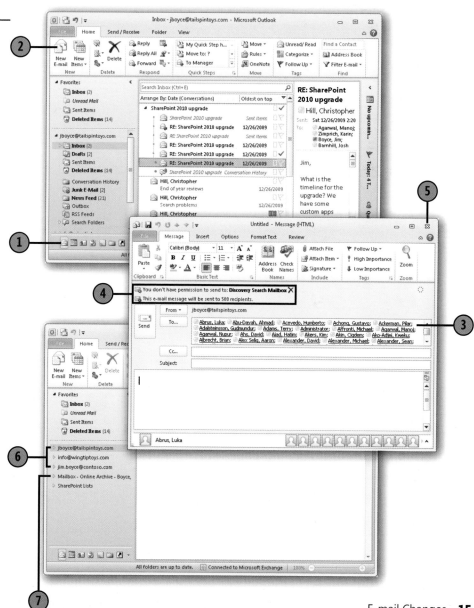

1. Click the Mail icon to open the Inbox.

2. Click New E-mail to start a new message.

3. Address the message to a large number of recipients.

4. Note that MailTips indicates that you're addressing the message to a large number of users, as well as other potential problems.

5. Close the message without sending it.

6. Note that Outlook can now include multiple Exchange Server accounts in one profile.

7. For Exchange Server 2010 accounts with online archive enabled, the archive shows up in the Navigation Pane.

Calendar Changes

You'll find some great new features in Outlook 2010 for managing your schedule, setting up meetings, and keeping track of other peoples' schedules, as well. For example, you can now preview meeting requests right in your Inbox, view your team members' and manager's free or busy time, and quickly create new calendar items from the ribbon.

① Click the Calendar icon in the Navigation Pane to display the Calendar folder.

② Click the Team branch in the Navigation Pane to view the free or busy information of people who report to you.

(continued on next page)

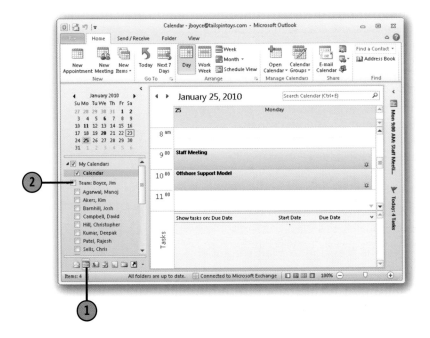

Tip

You can create your own custom calendar groups to show free or busy data for a group of people, whether they're in your management chain or not.

Calendar Changes *(continued)*

(3) Click your manager's team to view the free or busy information for everyone who reports to your manager (your peers).

(4) Click to open other calendars from your Exchange Server or from an Internet calendar sharing service.

(5) Click to publish your calendar at Office.com or at another calendar sharing service.

(6) Click the Mail icon to open the Inbox.

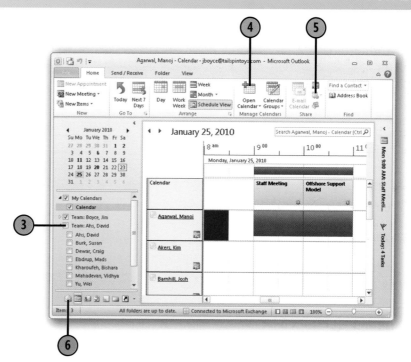

See Also

For information about working with tasks and the various task views, see "Viewing Your Tasks" on page 150.

Tip

The appearance of the Work Week and Week views are very similar, with the only difference being that Week view shows weekend days.

Meeting Preview

Another very handy new feature in Outlook 2010 lets you preview your calendar from your Inbox. When you receive a meeting invitation, Outlook displays a small snippet of your calendar so that you can see the requested meeting slot in context with the meetings and appointments adjacent to it.

(1) Click the Mail icon in the Navigation Pane to display the Inbox folder.

(2) Click a meeting invitation in the Inbox.

(3) In the Reading Pane, the meeting appears with the adjacent items.

(continued on next page)

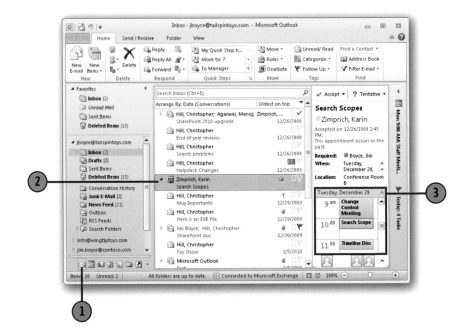

See Also

For information about scheduling meetings see "Setting Up a Meeting" on page 134.

Meeting Preview *(continued)*

④ Click Accept, and then click one of the following to:

⑤ Add notes to the reply and then send the response.

⑥ Send the response without adding notes.

⑦ Accept without sending a response.

⑧ Open a meeting invitation (must double-click).

⑨ View the meeting slot with adjacent items in the meeting request form.

⑩ Use these buttons to accept or decline.

⑪ Click Propose New Time if you want to propose a new time for the meeting.

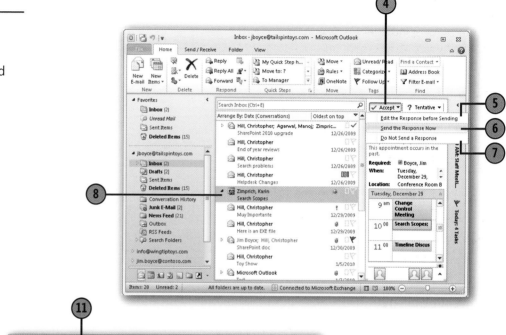

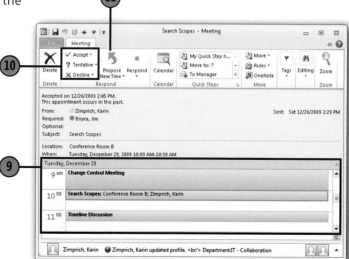

Easy Meeting Creation

Outlook 2010 adds some features to make it even easier to create new meeting requests. For example, you can create a meeting request from an e-mail with just a few clicks.

1. Click the Mail icon in the Navigation Pane to display the Inbox folder.

2. Click a message to select it.

3. Click the Reply With Meeting button in the ribbon.

4. The e-mail is added automatically to the meeting invitation.

5. The people in the e-mail conversation are added automatically to the meeting invitation list.

6. Enter a location.

7. Choose date and time.

8. Send the invitation.

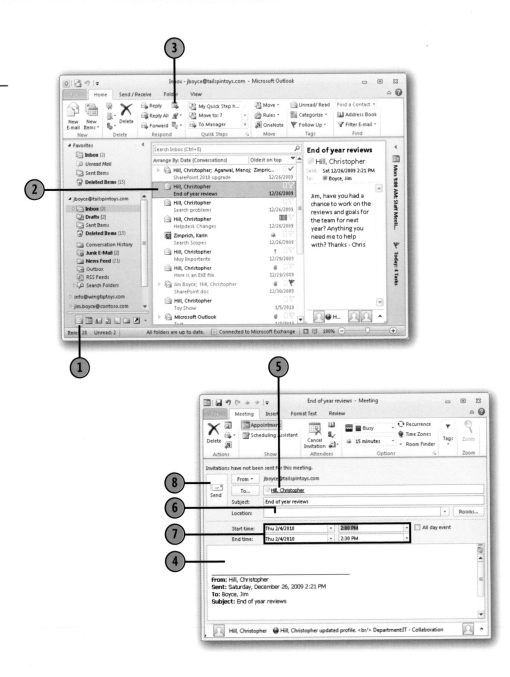

People and Presence

Previous versions of Outlook provided online presence information, enabling you to see at a glance when other users were online. Outlook 2010 expands presence capabilities and also adds new social network features.

Presence

Previous versions of Outlook worked in concert with Office Communicator to display an indicator of whether people were online. In Outlook 2010, enhanced presence enables you to see not only whether others are online, but also their availability for meetings and other information.

1. Click the Mail icon to open the Inbox.

2. Double-click to open a message.

3. Point to a contact.

4. A small contact card window pops up to display availability and other information.

5. Click to pin the contact open.

6. View the person's picture, if it's available.

7. Click to send an e-mail to the person.

8. Click to send an instant message to the person.

9. Click to start a voice conferencing call with the person.

10. Click to access other options, such as scheduling a meeting or viewing the person's My Site in SharePoint.

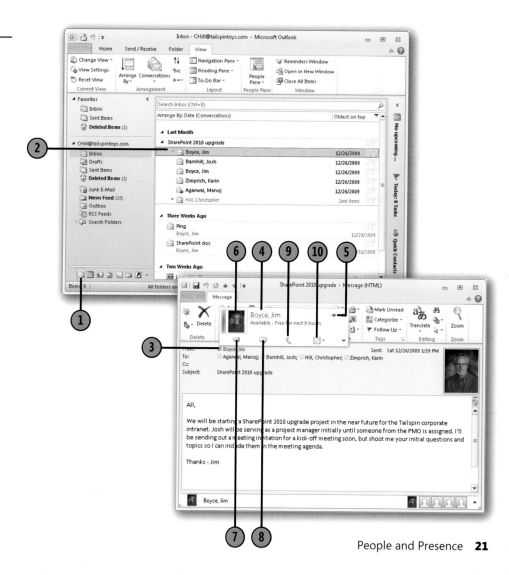

The People Pane

The People Pane is another Outlook 2010 new social networking feature that integrates information from Outlook and from external sources—SharePoint and social networking sites, such as LinkedIn, Windows Live, and so on. The items that come from Outlook include recent e-mails, attachments, and meetings. Status updates and activities come from the social networking sites to which you're connected.

1. Click the Mail icon to open the Inbox.
2. Click the View tab.
3. Click Reading Pane and choose Bottom.

(continued on next page)

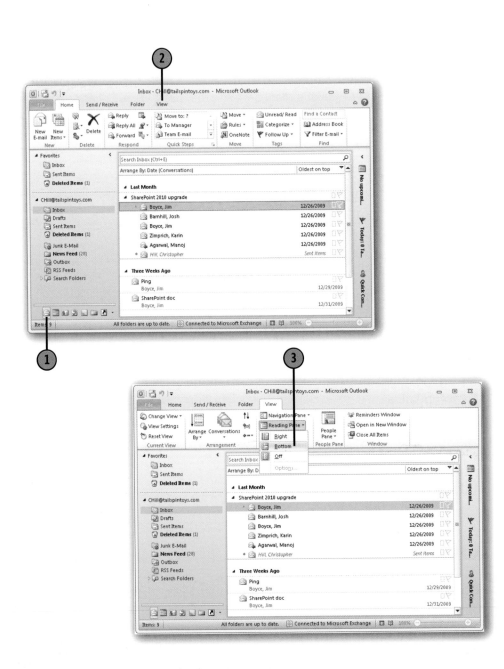

The People Pane *(continued)*

④ Click to expand the People Pane (if necessary).

⑤ Click to view recent e-mails from the person.

⑥ Click to view recent attachments.

⑦ Click to show scheduled meetings with the person.

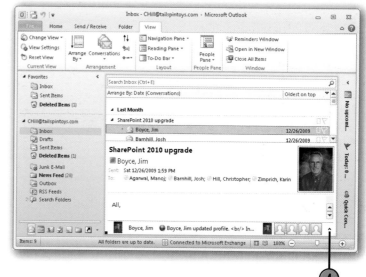

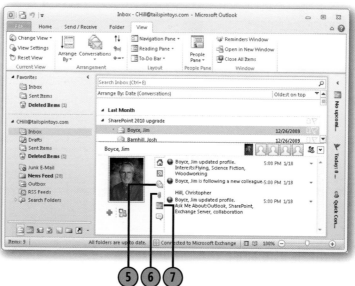

Search

The Outlook 2010 ribbon makes the program's search functions more easily accessible. You find the Search functions in the Search tab of the ribbon, which appears when you click inside the Search text box. The options in the Search tab offer various criteria to help you quickly refine your search.

1. Click the Mail icon to open the Inbox.

2. Click in the Search text box and type a search word or phrase.

3. Use the Scope group to specify where you want to search.

4. Use the Refine group to refine the search to specific criteria such as sender, subject, category, and so on.

(continued on next page)

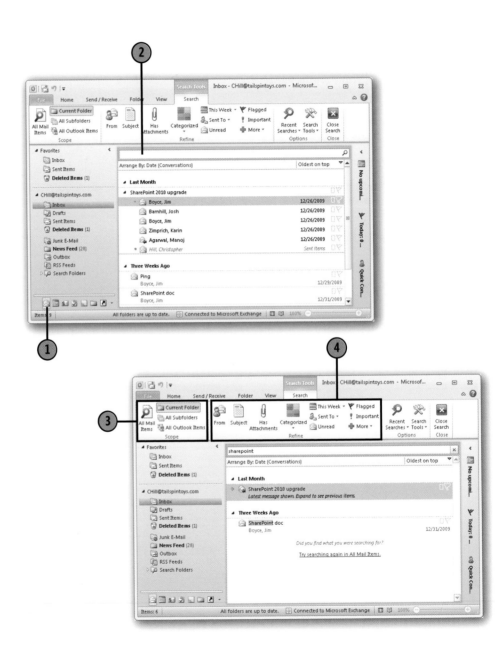

Search *(continued)*

⑤ Click More.

⑥ Choose additional criteria.

⑦ Click Recent Searches to view results from recent searches.

⑧ Click Search Tools to access other search options, including the Advanced Find dialog box.

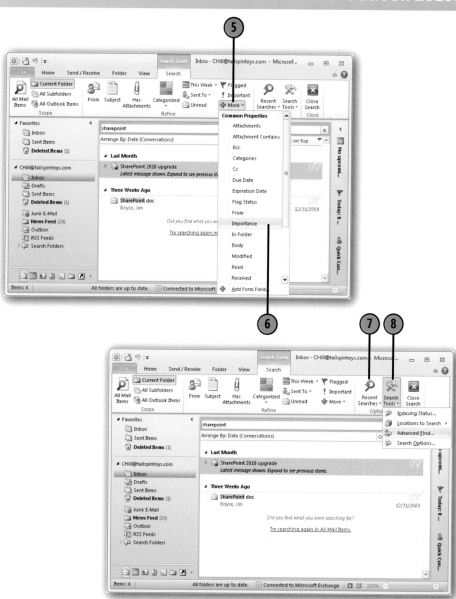

Mobility

Outlook 2010 offers some great features for integrating Outlook and your mobile device. If you're an Exchange Server 2010 user, you can configure your mailbox to have the server send alerts to your mobile device when you receive certain types of messages, notices for upcoming meetings, and so on. If you add an SMS provider, you can also send text messages from Outlook to other peoples' mobile devices.

Use Text Alerts

1. If you have an Exchange Server 2010 mailbox, click the File tab to open Backstage view.

2. Click Account Settings.

3. Choose Manage Mobile Notifications.

4. When prompted in Internet Explorer, provide your Exchange Server mailbox user name and password.

5. Click Sign In.

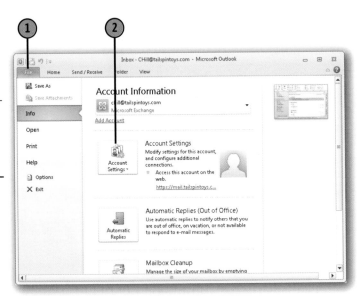

(continued on next page)

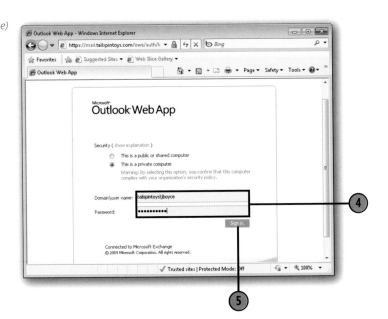

Use Text Alerts *(continued)*

⑥ Click the Phone link.

⑦ Click the Text Messaging icon.

⑧ Click the Set Up E-mail Notifications link.

⑨ Choose a rule condition.

⑩ Click More Options if you don't see the condition you want to use.

⑪ Choose Send A Text Message To.

⑫ Click the Select One link to choose your mobile device number.

⑬ Click Save.

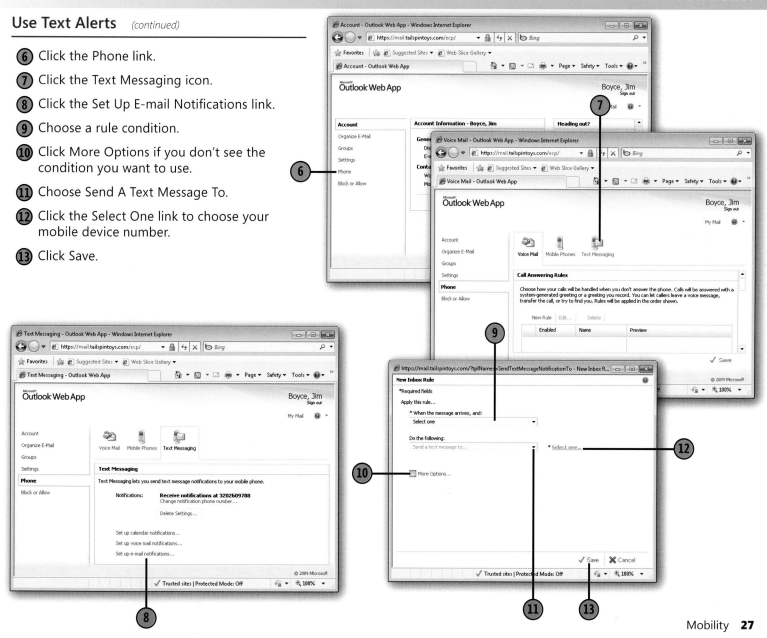

Send a Text Message

1. Click the Mail icon to open the Inbox.
2. After you have added an SMS provider to Outlook, click New Items.
3. Choose Text Message.
4. Click to choose a mobile recipient.
5. Or type a mobile device number in the text box.
6. Type the message you want to send.
7. Click Send.

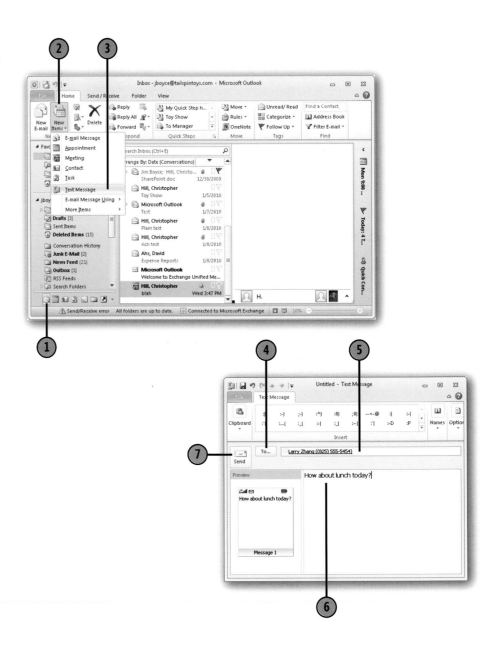

3

Getting Started

Microsoft Outlook 2010 can help you manage almost every aspect of your day. With Outlook, you have useful and manageable tools: your e-mail, contacts, calendar, and tasks. Using these tools, you can keep track even of your phone calls, time spent on documents, and other tasks and events.

Even with all of its many features, Outlook is easy to use. The program provides simple forms for creating and viewing messages, meetings, tasks, and other items. You can choose among several options for viewing your information in Outlook, and the program lets you customize the existing views and create new ones to give you exactly the view of your data that you need. With this book in hand, you can be up to speed with Outlook in just a few hours.

This section of the book offers a quick overview of Outlook and how to start using it. You learn how to open Outlook and how to move through the various folders it uses to store your data. You also learn how to work with Outlook items (such as messages, meetings, and contacts), import e-mail accounts and messages from other programs, and get help when you need more information about a particular feature or task.

Outlook 2010 at a Glance

At first, the Outlook program window can seem overwhelming to new users because it contains so much information. After you understand how Outlook organizes and presents that information, however, you have no trouble moving from folder to folder to view and arrange your information. The main program window organizes all of your Outlook folders for easy access, and individual windows help you work with the different types of Outlook items.

Overview of the Outlook Program Window

Outlook provides several folders and ways to view the contents of those folders. The default view is the Inbox view, which shows e-mail messages you have received.

Tip

If you need more space to display your schedule or other data, you can collapse the Navigation Pane or hide it altogether. Click the collapsed Navigation Pane or click Configure Buttons at the bottom of the Navigation pane to open a different Outlook folder.

See Also

The Inbox is the default view in Outlook, but you can choose a different view as your default view. See "Set the Startup View" on page 45 for details.

Perform common tasks with the Quick Access toolbar

Click other tabs to view additional options and commands

Select commands from the ribbon

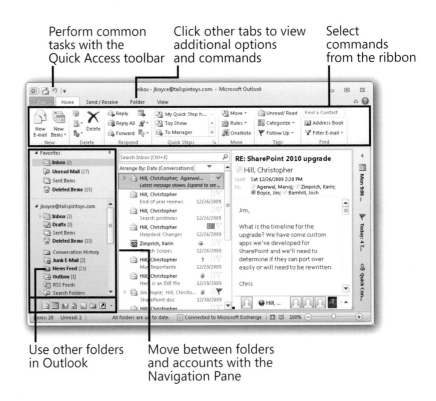

Use other folders in Outlook

Move between folders and accounts with the Navigation Pane

Overview of an Outlook Item Window

Each Outlook folder uses a different type of form to let you view, create, and work with items. Simply double-click an item to open its form, or click the small arrow beside the New Items command on the Standard toolbar and choose the type of item you want to create.

1. Click the New E-mail button to create a new item of the default type for the current folder.

2. Click the New Items button to select the type of item you want to create.

3. Double-click an item to open the item for viewing and editing.

4. View the opened item.

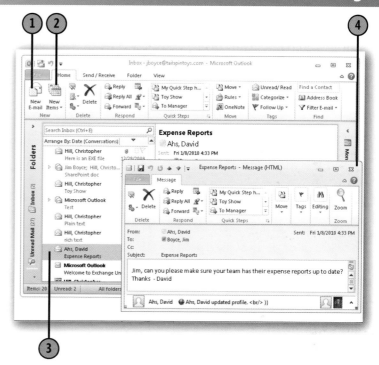

See Also

For information on customizing the Navigation Pane to add or remove icons, see "Customizing the Navigation Pane" on page 243.

Starting and Exiting Outlook

Before you can work with your Outlook items, you need to open Outlook. The program functions in much the same way as any other Windows program when it comes to starting, using, or exiting the program.

Start Outlook

① Click Start, All Programs, Microsoft Office, and then Microsoft Outlook 2010.

Tip

If you work with Outlook much of the day or every time you work on your computer, drag the Outlook icon from the Windows desktop to the All Programs/Startup folder on the Start menu to create a shortcut there for Outlook. Outlook then starts when you log on to your computer.

Try This!

Drag the Outlook icon from the Start menu to the desktop to give you an easy way to open Outlook from the desktop.

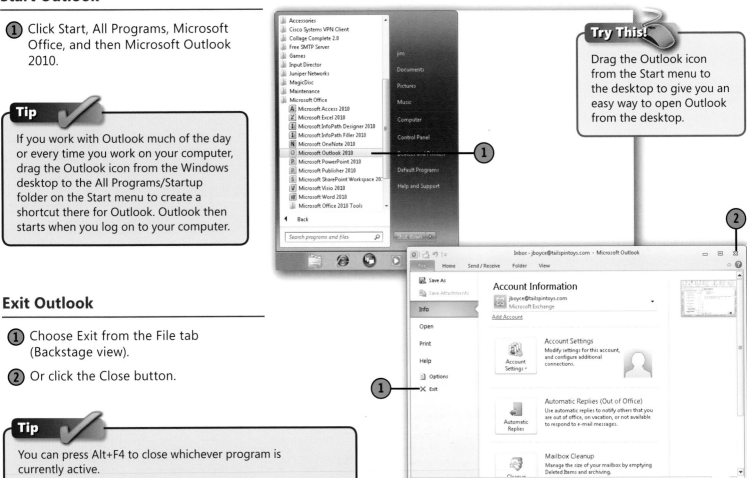

Exit Outlook

① Choose Exit from the File tab (Backstage view).

② Or click the Close button.

Tip

You can press Alt+F4 to close whichever program is currently active.

Exploring Outlook Folders

Outlook includes several folders that contain different types of data. The Inbox receives incoming messages, and outgoing messages depart through the Outbox. The Drafts folder holds messages that you're working on, and the Sent Items folder keeps a copy of each message you send. You can use the Contacts folder to store contact information and the Calendar folder to store your schedule. The Navigation Pane and the Folder list give you quick access to your folders.

Use the Navigation Pane

① Click the Mail icon to open the Inbox folder.

② Click the root of your default e-mail account to open the Outlook Today view.

③ Click other icons to open items not shown on the Navigation Pane.

Use the Folder List

① Click the Folder List icon.

② Drag the resizing bar down to show more of the folder list.

③ Click a white triangle to expand a folder's listing.

④ Click a black triangle to collapse a folder's listing.

⑤ Click a folder to open it in Outlook.

⑥ Click a different icon to display that folder's contents.

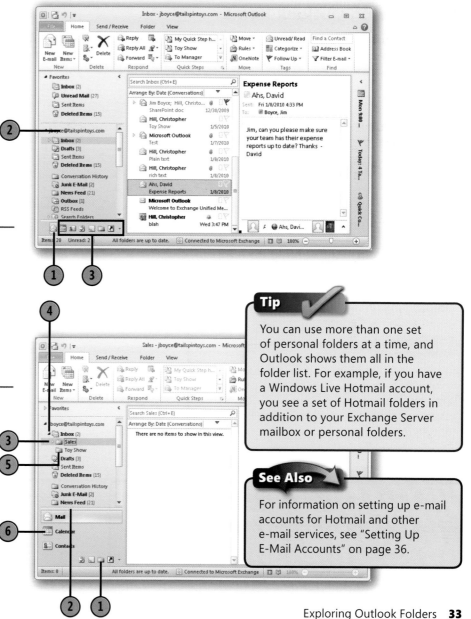

Tip

You can use more than one set of personal folders at a time, and Outlook shows them all in the folder list. For example, if you have a Windows Live Hotmail account, you see a set of Hotmail folders in addition to your Exchange Server mailbox or personal folders.

See Also

For information on setting up e-mail accounts for Hotmail and other e-mail services, see "Setting Up E-Mail Accounts" on page 36.

Working with Outlook Items

Outlook helps you store information and send messages a variety of ways. You can use messages, contacts, journal entries, tasks, appointments, meetings, and notes, each of which constitutes a type of Outlook item. Outlook stores each type in a particular folder and presents the information in a way that makes the most sense for that type of data. In many situations, you can retrieve the information you need simply by opening the folder without actually opening the item.

Review Items in a Folder

1. In the Navigation Pane, click the folder whose contents you want to view.

2. Use the scroll bar to view additional items.

3. View the item in the Reading Pane.

4. In the Contacts folder, click the letter that corresponds to the first initial of other names you want to view.

Tip

The Reading Pane appears below or to the right of the contents pane and displays the contents of an item when you click it. To open the Reading Pane—or to close it—choose Reading Pane from the View tab.

Tip

Outlook provides an AutoPreview option for list views such as the default Inbox, Tasks, and Notes folder views. When Auto-Preview is turned on, Outlook displays the first few lines of the item below the item's header. To turn AutoPreview on or off, choose Preview from the Change View item on the View tab.

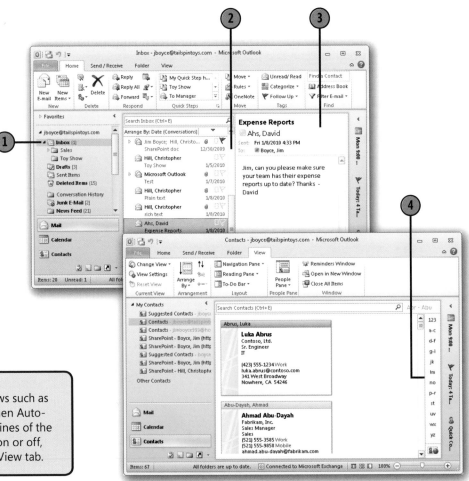

Open an Item

1 In the Navigation Pane, click the folder containing the item you want to open.

2 Locate the item in the contents pane, and double-click it.

3 View the item in its current form, or make changes as necessary.

4 Click the Save & Close button to save your changes to the item and close the form.

5 Or click Close to close the form without making changes.

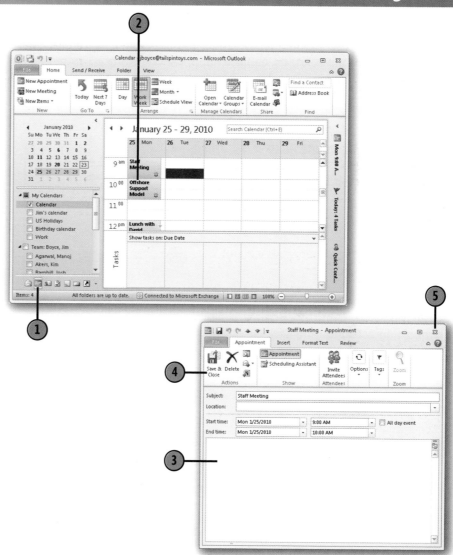

Setting Up E-Mail Accounts

You can use Outlook to send and receive messages for several different types of e-mail accounts. Outlook supports Microsoft Exchange Server; POP3 services, such as a typical account from an Internet service provider (ISP); IMAP services; and Windows Live Hotmail (with the Outlook Connector installed). You can easily add a new account or import e-mail account settings from Microsoft Outlook Express, Windows Mail, or Eudora. (Outlook 2010 does not support imports from applications such as Netscape or Firefox. It also does not import mail settings from Windows Live Mail.)

Import E-Mail Accounts

1. Open Outlook, and click the File tab.

2. Click Open.

3. Click Import.

4. Choose Import Internet Mail Account Settings.

5. Click Next.

6. Select the program from which you're importing accounts, and click Next.

(continued on next page)

Try This!

Entering your e-mail address on Web sites is a good way to fill your Inbox with spam, but some sites require your address when you register. One option is to set up an Internet mail address with Hotmail or one of the other providers, and use this exclusively for password verification. That way the unsolicited e-mail goes to an address that you check only occasionally.

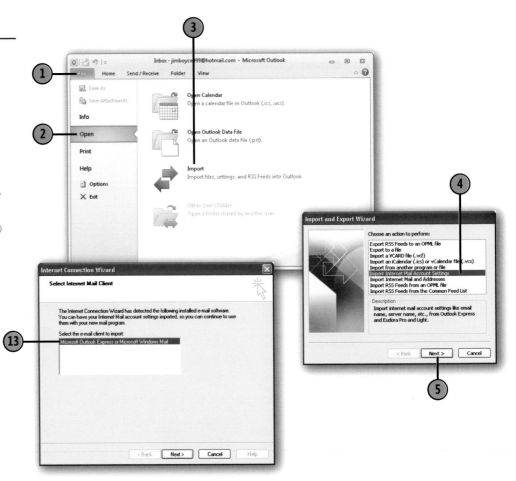

Import E-Mail Accounts *(continued)*

⑦ Verify or change your name in the account, and click Next.

⑧ Verify or change your e-mail address for the account, and click Next.

⑨ Verify the server type, incoming and outgoing mail server addresses, and click Next.

⑩ Verify or change the account name.

⑪ Set the password, and click Next.

⑫ Select the type of connection to use for the account, click Next, and then click Finish.

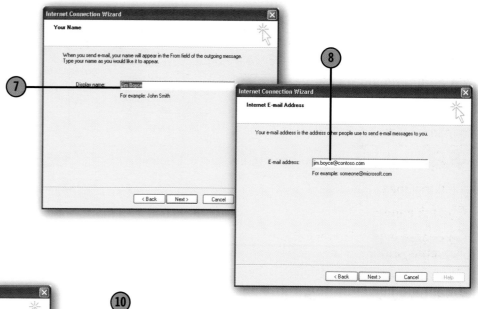

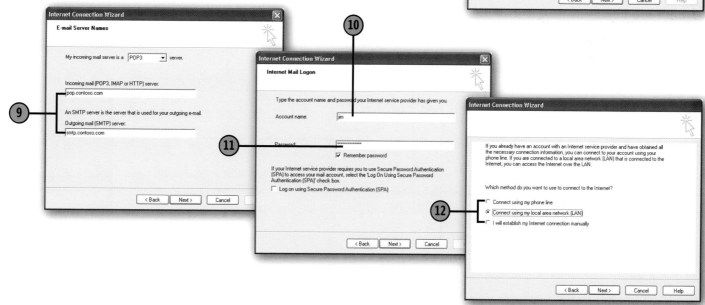

Add an E-Mail Account Manually

① Click the File tab.

② Click Account Settings.

③ Click Account Settings.

④ Click New.

⑤ Select E-mail Account.

⑥ Click Next.

(continued on next page)

Tip

You can add, change, and remove Outlook e-mail accounts, personal folders, address books, RSS feeds, SharePoint lists, and directory services through the Mail icon in Windows Control Panel.

Try This!

Outlook can often add e-mail accounts automatically. In the Add New Account dialog box, fill in your name, e-mail address, and password, and click Next. Outlook attempts to identify the mail server based on your e-mail address and performs some tests to verify that it can send and receive using the specified server. If Outlook can't determine the right settings, Outlook prompts you to enter them manually.

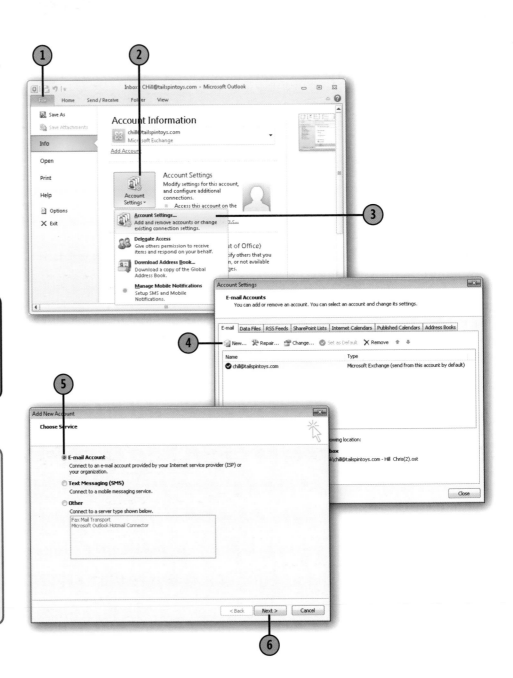

Add an E-Mail Account
Manually *(continued)*

(7) Select Manually Configure Server Settings Or Additional Server Types, and then click Next.

(8) Select Internet E-mail, and click Next.

(9) Type your name and e-mail address.

(10) Choose the account type.

(11) Type the incoming and outgoing mail server names provided by your ISP or e-mail administrators.

(12) Type your user name and password for the server account you're testing.

(13) Click Test Account Settings to have Outlook test your settings, and then close the test window when the test is completed successfully. Click Next and Finish to return to the Account Settings window.

See Also

For information on keeping messages from different accounts separated from one another, see "Working with the Rules Wizard" on page 86.

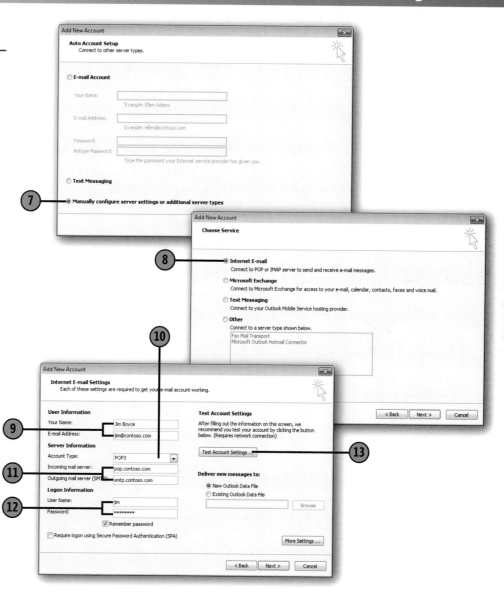

Importing Data from Another Program

If you switch to Outlook from Outlook Express, Windows Mail, or Eudora, you might want to import your existing messages and contacts so that you can continue working with them.

Importing messages, addresses, and data into Outlook saves the time you'd need to re-create them manually.

Retrieve Internet Mail and Addresses

① Click the File tab.

② Click Open.

③ Click Import.

④ Select Import Internet Mail And Addresses and click Next.

⑤ Select the program from which you're importing items.

⑥ Select the types of items you want to import, and click Next.

⑦ Specify how you want Outlook to treat duplicate items, and then click Finish.

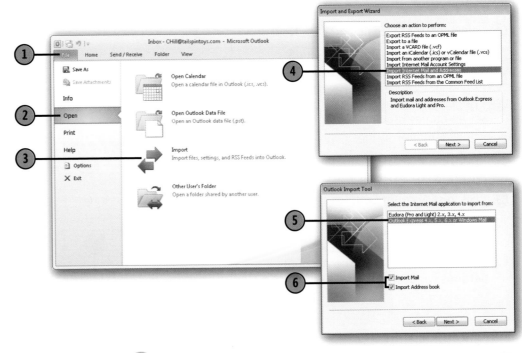

Tip ✓

Outlook 2010 automatically detects existing accounts the first time you start Oulook and asks whether you want to import the accounts. Use this method only if you previously directed Outlook not to import existing accounts for you.

Retrieve Data from Another Program

1. Click the File tab.
2. Choose Open.
3. Click Import.
4. Select Import From Another Program Or File, and click Next.
5. Select the file type of the data you want to import.
6. Click Next.

(continued on next page)

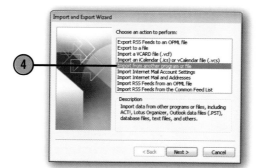

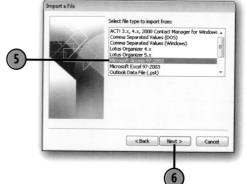

Tip

When you import data from certain programs, you might need to perform some additional steps when bringing the data into Outlook. For example, if you're importing contacts from Excel, you might need to map the columns in Excel to fields in the Outlook contact item.

Retrieve Data from Another
Program *(continued)*

7 Click Browse to locate the file, or type the file path and name in the File To Import text box.

8 Choose how you want Outlook to treat duplicate data, and then click Next.

9 Select the Outlook folder in which you want Outlook to store the imported items, and click Next.

10 Place a check mark beside each item you want to import. If the Map Custom Fields dialog box doesn't open, click Map Custom Fields.

11 Click and drag an item from the From list to the To list and drop it on the Outlook field to which you want the item copied. This action tells Outlook where to place the incoming data. Repeat for all items to be imported, and then click OK.

12 Click Finish when you're ready to import the data.

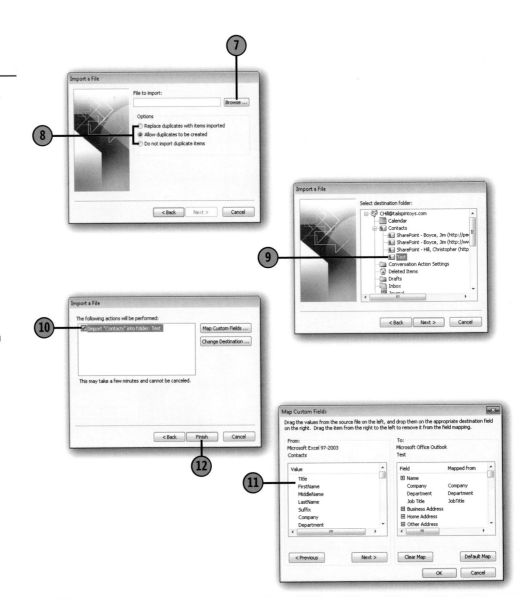

Viewing Items and Folders

Outlook offers several different views, depending on the folder you open. You can use the default views to work with the data in the folder or change the view to tailor it to your needs. The Outlook Today view gives you a single place to view your pending appointments, tasks, and messages, giving you a summary of your workday or workweek. You can also use the View tab to switch easily among the available views for a particular Outlook folder.

Use the Outlook Today View

1 In Outlook, click the e-mail address for the account you want to work with in the Navigation Pane.

2 To open an appointment, click the appointment in the Calendar list.

3 Select the check box beside a task to mark it as complete.

4 Click a task to open the task.

5 Click the Inbox or other folder to open the folder and work with your messages.

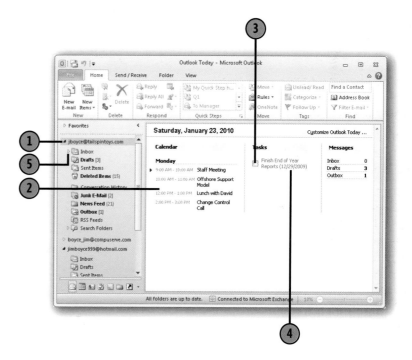

Use the Current View Menu

① In Outlook, select the folder you want to view.

② Click the View tab.

③ Click Change View.

④ Choose a view.

Try This!

Open the Contacts folder and click New in the ribbon to create a new contact. Fill in the fields on the General page, and click Save & Close to save the contact. With the Contacts folder open, click the View tab, click Change View, and then select Card. Outlook displays more information in the Contacts folder. Click Change View, and then select Phone to change to a view that is handy for quickly locating phone numbers.

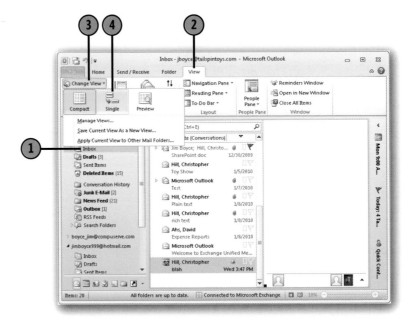

Set the Startup View

1. In Outlook, click the File tab.
2. Click Options.
3. Click Advanced to show the Advanced page of the Outlook Options dialog box.
4. Click Browse, and choose the folder you want Outlook to display when you first start the program.
5. Click OK to close the Options dialog box.

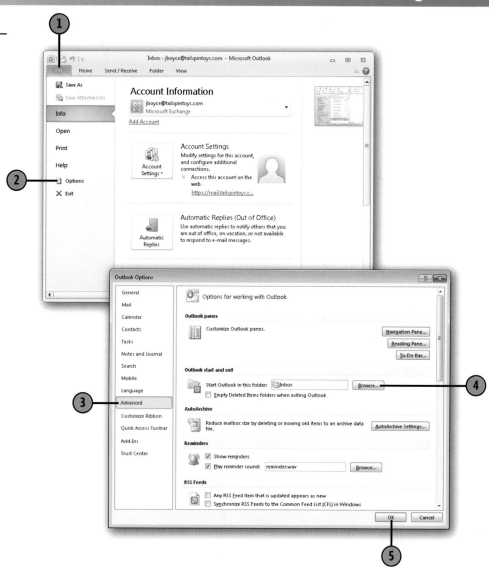

Getting Help in Outlook 2010

Every new program has a learning curve. Getting up to speed with Outlook can take some time because of the number of features it offers. Even after you become comfortable using Outlook every day, you're likely to need some help with features you've never used before or those you seldom use. Outlook provides extensive help documentation though. You can access this information in a couple of ways.

Use Outlook Help Content

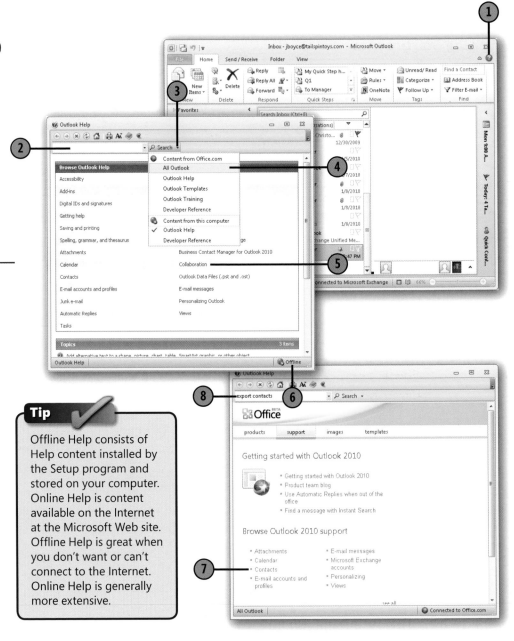

1. Click the Question Mark button above the ribbon.

2. Click in the text box, and type a word or phrase.

3. Click the arrow beside the Search button.

4. Choose where to search for the information.

5. Click a topic heading to view related topics.

6. Click to choose between online and offline Help content.

7. Click a topic to browse for support.

8. Or enter a search word or phrase and click Search.

Tip

Offline Help consists of Help content installed by the Setup program and stored on your computer. Online Help is content available on the Internet at the Microsoft Web site. Offline Help is great when you don't want or can't connect to the Internet. Online Help is generally more extensive.

Writing and Sending E-Mail

Microsoft Outlook 2010 handles many daily tasks for you, such as keeping your calendar, collecting notes, and saving your contacts. But the main feature of Outlook is its electronic mail (e-mail) features. Outlook is often referred to as a universal inbox—it can send, receive, and store messages from a number of different e-mail sources. These sources can include internal networks, Internet e-mail accounts, and other sources.

The e-mail features in Outlook enable you to create e-mail messages and send them to other users. With the help of the Outlook Address Book, you can quickly access a recipient's e-mail address when you're ready to address your new e-mail message. Outlook also provides ways to send one message to multiple users using contract groups, format e-mail message text to contain rich content (such as hypertext) and to use HTML stationery, and use signatures at the bottom of all your outgoing messages.

In this section, you learn how to write and modify e-mail messages, send messages, and review messages you've already sent. In addition, you learn how to use the Address Book to select recipient names, create and use contact groups, format your messages, use signatures, send attached files, and work with HTML stationery.

Writing an E-Mail Message

When you write new messages in Outlook, you use the Message window. This window has a line for recipients (called the To line), a line for "carbon copied" recipients (the Cc line), a Subject line, and an area for the text of the message. Every new message must have at least one recipient. If you want, you can leave the Cc and Subject lines blank, but it's a good idea to give your messages a subject.

Address an E-Mail Message

1. In Outlook, click New E-mail on the Home tab of the ribbon to display a new Message window.

2. To open the Select Names dialog box, click To.

3. Click the Address Book drop-down arrow.

4. Click the name of the address book you want to use, such as Contacts. The addresses in the selected address book appear in the box.

5. Click the name of the person to whom you want to send the new message.

6. Click To, Cc, or Bcc; Outlook copies the name to the specified message recipients list.

7. Repeat steps 5 and 6 until the message recipients list includes all the recipients you want to send the message to.

8. Click OK.

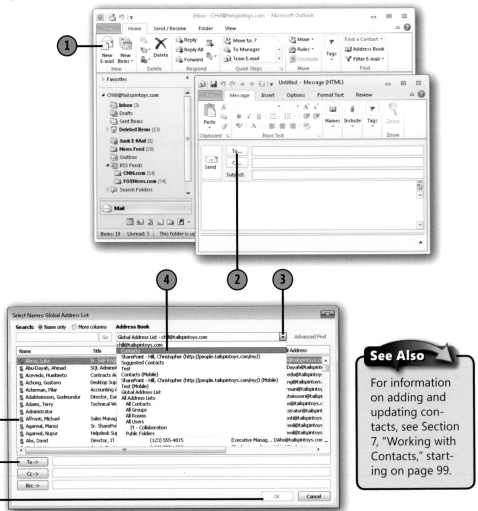

See Also

For information on adding and updating contacts, see Section 7, "Working with Contacts," starting on page 99.

Type Your Message Subject and Text

(1) In the new Message window, type a subject for the new message in the Subject field.

(2) Press Tab or click in the message body area.

(3) Type your message.

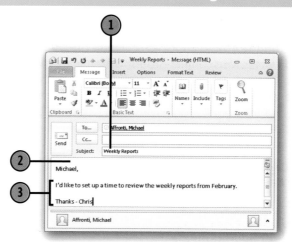

Tip

As you write your message, you do not have to press Enter at the end of each line. Keep typing and Outlook wraps the text to the next line. To create a new paragraph, press Enter. If you want each paragraph to be separated by two blank lines, press Enter twice at the end of each paragraph. This makes your messages easier to read than single-spaced messages.

See Also

After you type your message, you can send it. Sending messages is discussed later in "Sending Messages" on page 66.

Caution

You can apply special formatting to your message (see "Formatting Message Text" on page 57), but you might not want to. If you send mail to people who use a different e-mail program, they might not see the formatting that you intended. When in doubt, it's usually a good policy to keep your messages simple so that nothing gets lost in the translation.

Working with the Address Book

You can use the Outlook Address Book to search for and select names, e-mail addresses, and contact groups. When you type a recipient name in the To field of the Message window, Outlook searches the Address Book for a match. The Address Book gives you access to any address books you have set up (see the Tip about address books below), as well as information from the Contacts folder, Microsoft Exchange Server Global Address List (if you have an Exchange Server mailbox), and Internet directory services. Depending on the way you have Outlook set up, you may have information from only one of these sources, or you may have contact information from multiple types.

Open the Address Book

1. In Outlook, click Address Book in the Find group on the Home tab.

2. Click the selection arrow on the Address Book drop-down list.

3. Click the address book from which you want to view addresses.

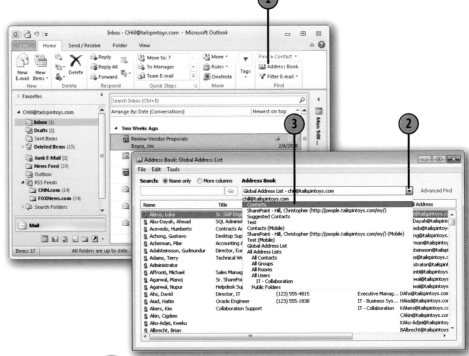

See Also

For more on working with your contact information, see Section 7, "Working with Contacts," starting on page 99.

Tip

You can set up several different address books to store your e-mail recipients' contact information. For example, you might have a company-wide address book that stores addresses and contact information for all internal employees. A second address book can be set up for external contacts, such as vendors, suppliers, and customers. A third address book could store personal contact information.

Tip

If your installation of Outlook is not set up for other address books, such as an Exchange Server Global Address List, the only address book you can select from the drop-down list is the Outlook Contacts folder, which appears as "Contacts" under your e-mail account. Note that the Outlook Address Book collects together all address books, but is not an address book itself in the sense that it stores addresses. Instead, it shows addresses from multiple address books.

Find a Name in the Address Book

1. In the Address Book dialog box, click in the Search text box.

2. Type the name of the contact you want to find.

3. The first contact that matches is highlighted in the list of names.

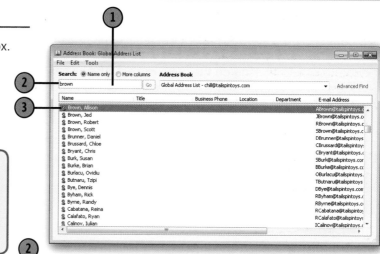

Try This!

Assume you want to find a contact whose name is Dave. You're not sure whether you listed him as "Dave" or "David" in your Contacts folder. To find him, in your Address Book choose Find from the Tools menu, type **dav**, and press Enter. Outlook displays all names containing "dav", such as "Dave," "Davey," "David," and so on.

Tip

If you want to redisplay your entire address book after a search, select an address book from the Address Book drop-down list and click Name Only. Notice that Outlook now lists search results as a selection in case you want to return to your latest search results.

E-Mail a Name in the Address Book

1. In the Address Book dialog box, click a contact to whom you want to send an e-mail message.

2. Choose New Message from the File menu.

3. Type a subject.

4. Type your message text in the message body area.

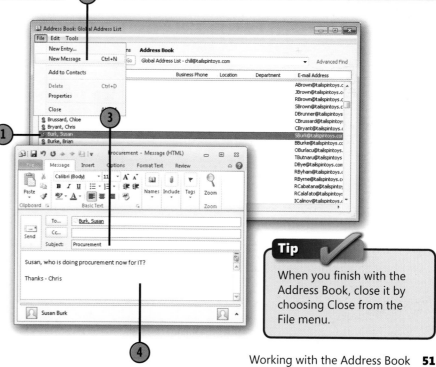

Tip

When you finish with the Address Book, close it by choosing Close from the File menu.

Working with Contact Groups

A contract group is a group of contacts that are related in some way. For example, you could create a contact group that includes contacts working on the same project. Then when you need to send messages to the entire project team, simply select the contact group for that project; Outlook sends the message to all the contacts in the group. Contact groups are stored in the Contacts folder by default. Contact groups are also referred to as distribution lists.

Create a Contact Group

1. In Outlook, click New Items from Home tab on the ribbon.

2. Click More Items and choose Contact Group from the submenu.

3. Click in the Name field and type a name for the new contact group.

4. Click Add Members in the ribbon and choose From Address Book to open the Select Members dialog box.

(continued on next page)

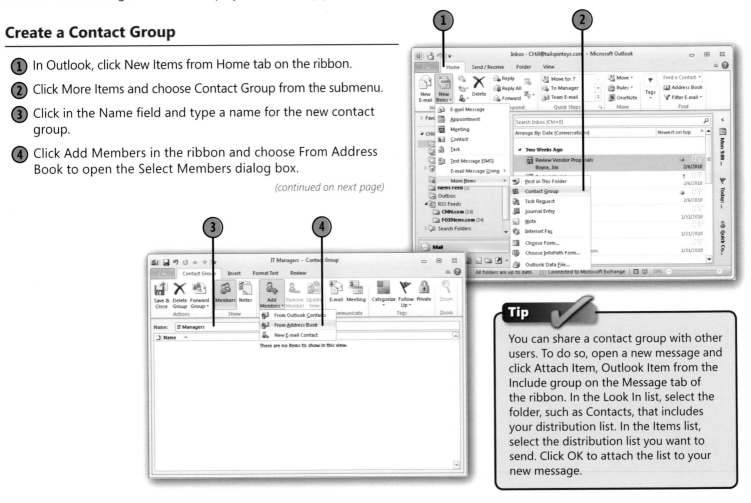

Tip

You can share a contact group with other users. To do so, open a new message and click Attach Item, Outlook Item from the Include group on the Message tab of the ribbon. In the Look In list, select the folder, such as Contacts, that includes your distribution list. In the Items list, select the distribution list you want to send. Click OK to attach the list to your new message.

Create a Contact Group *(continued)*

(5) From the Address Book drop-down list, select the address book that contains the names you want to add to the distribution list.

(6) Click in the Search text box and type a name you want to add to the distribution list, or choose a name from the list that appears in the Name field.

(7) Click Members to copy the name to the address list text box.

(8) Click OK when your list is complete.

(9) Click Save & Close.

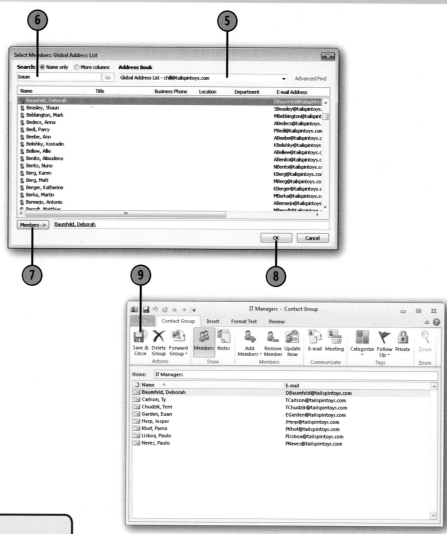

Tip

You can add existing contacts to a contact group, and also add other addresses for recipients who are not among your existing contacts.

Use a Contact Group

(1) In Outlook, click New E-mail on the Home tab of the ribbon to start a new e-mail message.

(2) Click To.

(3) From the Name list, click the contact group you want to use to address your e-mail message.

(4) Click To.

(5) Click OK.

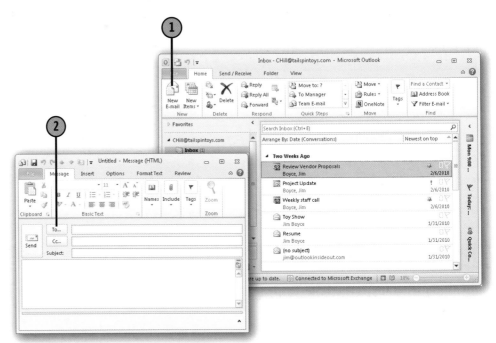

Caution

When you use a contact group, everyone on the list receives the same message. If you want to send a message to only a select few on the list, such as a confidential message that only specific recipients should read, create a new contact group for these recipients, or select the recipients individually in the Select Names dialog box.

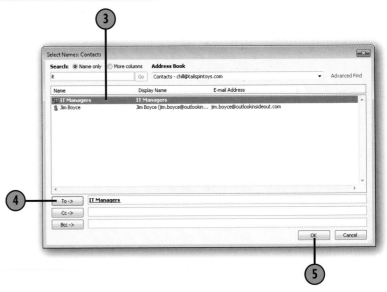

Changing a Message Before Sending

After you create a message and before you send it, you should proofread it for errors or omissions. If you discover a typographical or other error, you can edit it in the same way you would a word-processing document. You can use familiar commands like Copy and Paste or operations like dragging to edit your text.

Edit Your Message

① In Outlook, create a new mail message with recipients, a subject, and message text.

② To change the recipient, click To.

③ In the Select Names dialog box, click a name in the Name list and click To, which adds it to the Message Recipients list.

④ Click a name in the To list and press Delete or Backspace to remove that person from the list.

⑤ Continue adding or deleting recipients until your recipient list includes all those you want to send the message to.

⑥ Click OK.

⑦ Click in the Subject line where you want to change text.

⑧ Click in the message body area where you want to change text.

⑨ Add or delete text as needed.

See Also

If you need to modify a contact's information, such as the e-mail address or name, you can do so in the Contacts folder. See "Updating an Existing Contact" on page 111.

Move and Copy Message Text

① Display the message containing the text you want to move or copy.

② Select the text you want to move or copy.

③ Drag the text to a new location. Or, to copy the text, hold down the Ctrl key as you drag the text.

④ Drop the text.

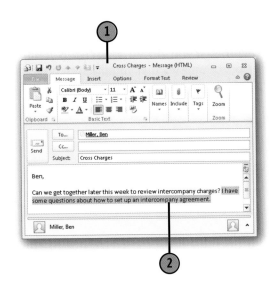

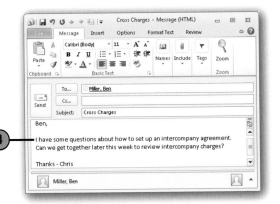

Tip

Message text can be moved or copied within a message, from one message to another, and between Outlook and other applications. For example, if you have a selection of text you want to use in several messages, you can select the text and press Ctrl+C to copy the text to the Clipboard, click in the body of each new message, and press Ctrl+V to paste the text into each message. You can also use the Copy and Paste buttons on the Message tab of the ribbon to copy and paste text.

Try This!

You can drag text from one message to another. Open both messages and position them so you can see both windows. Select the text you want to move and drag it to the other message window. Release the mouse button.

Formatting Message Text

Outlook lets you format text so that it looks more attractive to you and your recipients. For example, you can apply bold, italic, underline, colors, and other rich formatting to your messages.

You also can add HTML formatting to your messages, including tables, hyperlinks, heading levels, and more.

Use a Rich Text or HTML Message Format

 Create a new message, and add some text.

 Click the Format Text tab in the ribbon.

 Choose HTML or Rich Text from the Format group on the ribbon.

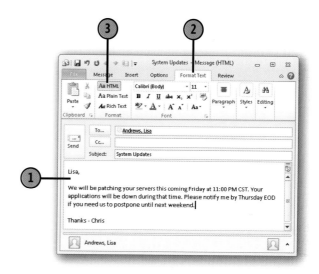

 **Tip**

Outlook 2010 uses Microsoft Word as the e-mail editor. There is no built-in Outlook editor as in Outlook 2003 or earlier.

Caution

If you add a hyperlink to a message, your recipient needs access to that site or document. For example, if the document you specify in the hyperlink is on the Internet, your recipient must have Internet access. Likewise, if your link is to a document you have stored locally on your hard drive, your recipient must have share privileges to that document.

Caution

Some recipients may not be able to handle rich-formatted text. In these cases, the formatted text you see in your message window appears to your recipients as plain text or is converted to unrecognizable characters.

Tip

To add a hyperlink to an e-mail message, type the hyperlink in your message and Outlook converts it to a live link that your recipient can click. For example, you can add a hyperlink to the Microsoft Web site by typing *www.microsoft.com* in your message.

Add Formatting to a Message

① Select the text you want to format.

② Click the Format Text tab on the ribbon.

③ Click Bold in the Font group to bold the text.

④ Click Italic to italicize the text.

⑤ Click Underline to underline the text.

⑥ Select a font name from the Font drop-down list to change the text font.

⑦ Select a color from the Font Color drop-down list to change the text font color.

⑧ Select a value from the Font Size drop-down list to change the text font size.

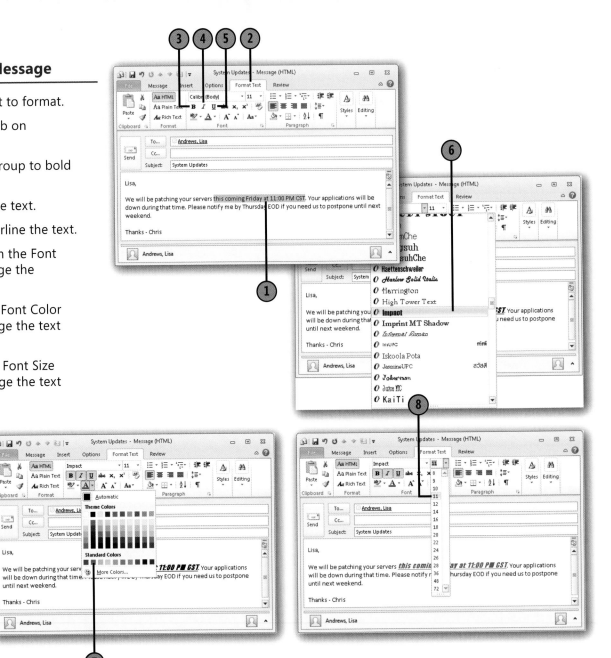

Using Signatures

A signature is boilerplate text or an image that's attached to any new messages you compose. The signature appears at the bottom of your messages. Many people include phone numbers and other information in their signatures.

Create a Signature

1. In Outlook, click the File tab.
2. Click Options.
3. In the Options dialog box, click Mail.
4. Click Signatures to open the Signatures And Stationery dialog box.

(continued on next page)

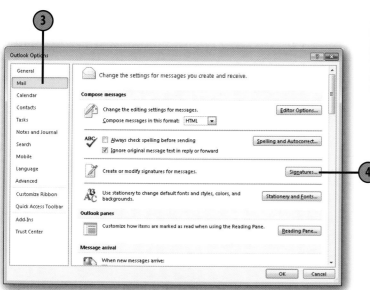

Tip

Business signatures frequently include the signer's name, title, company name, address, phone number, and e-mail address.

Create a Signature *(continued)*

⑤ Click New to open the New Signature dialog box.

⑥ Type a name for the signature and click OK.

⑦ Choose a font and font size.

⑧ Select font format options.

⑨ In the Edit Signature field, type the text you want to appear in your signature.

⑩ Add pictures or links to the signature, if you want.

⑪ Click OK twice to save your signature.

Tip

You can create custom signatures for the type of e-mail message you create. For example, you can create a friendly signature for messages intended for family or friends, and a more formal one for business recipients.

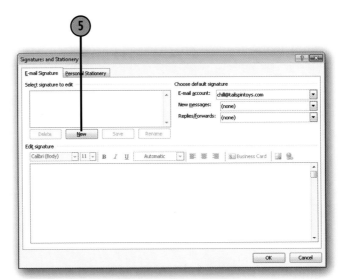

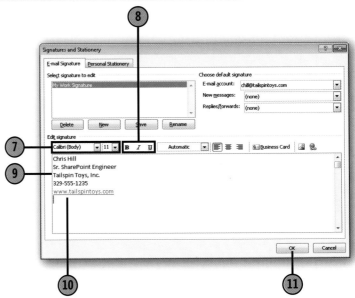

Choose a Signature

1. In Outlook, click the File tab, Options, and then click Mail.

2. Click Signatures to open the Signatures And Stationery dialog box.

3. From the E-mail Account drop-down list, select the account for which you want to assign the signature.

4. Select a signature from the New Messages drop-down list.

5. Click OK, then click OK to close the Options dialog box.

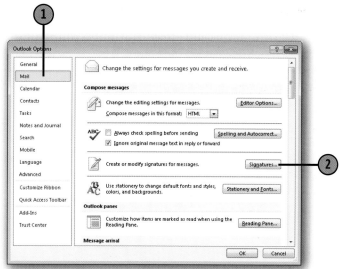

Tip

If you want your signature to appear in messages you reply to or forward, select the appropriate signature from the Replies/Forwards drop-down list.

See Also

For information on replying to and forwarding messages, see "Replying to and Forwarding E-Mail" on page 81.

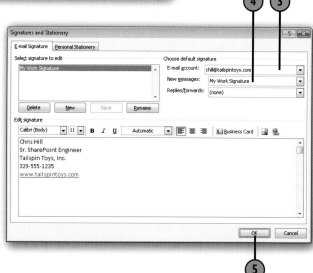

Working with HTML Stationery

Outlook includes a set of predefined designs and color schemes you can add to your rich text-formatted messages. These are known as HTML stationery. You can use or modify the stationery Outlook provides. When you create a message, you can specify which stationery you want to use or set Outlook to use a default stationery pattern each time you create a new message. You can also specify the background image or color for an individual message.

Select Stationery

① In Outlook, open the Inbox and click New Items, and then click E-mail Message Using.

② Choose More Stationery from the submenu.

③ Choose the stationery you want for your new message from the Theme Or Stationery dialog box.

④ Click OK.

> **Tip** ✔
>
> You can also use Office themes for messages. To do so, click the Themes button on the Options tab in the message form's ribbon. You can then select an existing theme from the gallery, browse for themes, save the current them, or search the Microsoft Office Online Web site for more themes.

> **Caution** !
>
> To use HTML stationery, your message must be in HTML format. Your recipients' e-mail programs must be able to read this type of formatting or your e-mail recipients won't be able to see the stationery or any other formatting on your page.

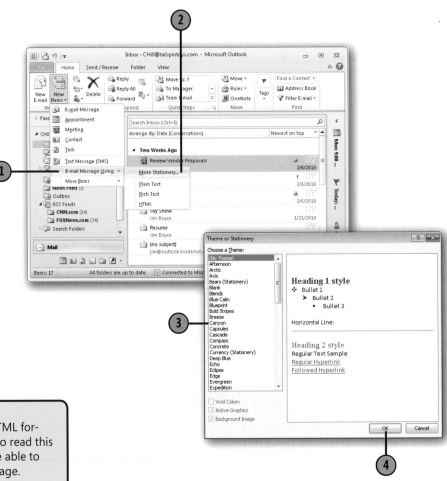

Edit Stationery

(1) Click the File tab, Options, and then click Mail.

(2) Click Stationery And Fonts to open the Signatures And Stationery dialog box.

(3) Click Theme, choose the stationery you want to edit, and then click OK.

(4) From the Font drop-down list, choose Always Use My Fonts.

(5) Choose the font options you want to modify.

(6) Click OK.

See Also

To learn how to change to HTML formatting, see "Use a Rich Text or HTML Message Format" on page 57.

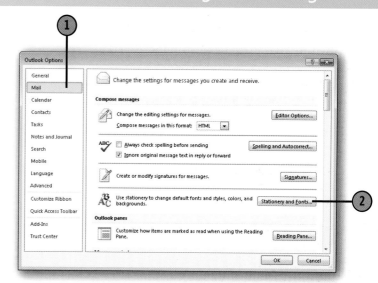

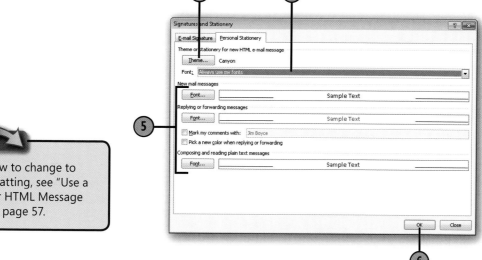

E-Mailing a File

Sometimes when you create an e-mail message, you want to send along a file as well. Files sent with e-mail are called message attachments. When you send the message, the file goes along with the message; the recipient can open it on his or her computer. Outlook also allows you to insert pictures into your e-mail messages.

Insert a Picture

1. To insert a picture in a message, you must choose either HTML or Rich Text format for the message. Open the message into which you want to insert a picture, and then choose HTML or Rich Text from the Format group of the Format Text tab on the ribbon.

2. Click in the body of the message

3. Click the Insert tab on the ribbon.

4. Click Picture to open the Insert Picture dialog box.

5. Choose the picture you want to insert.

6. Click Insert.

7. The picture is now part of the message.

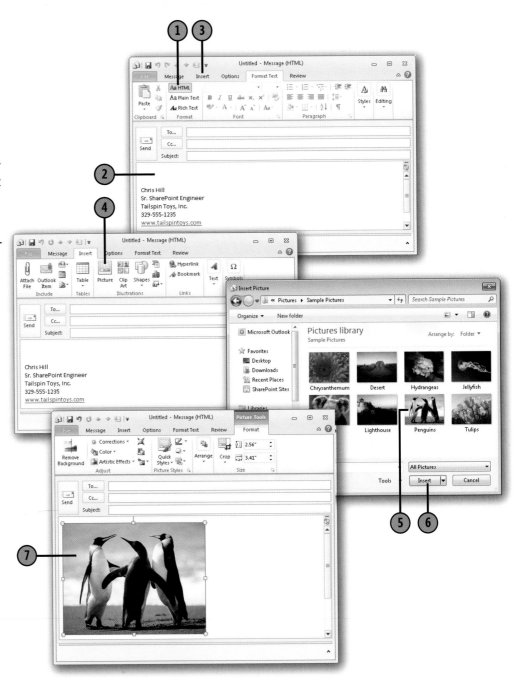

Attach a File

1. Open a new message, and click the Insert tab on the ribbon.
2. Click Attach File in the Include group.
3. Click the file you want to attach.
4. Click Insert.

Caution

The recipient of an attached file must have an application on his or her computer that can open the attached file. If not, you may need to save the file in an agreed-on format before sending the file.

See Also

For information on saving and opening file attachments you receive from other people, see "Working with Attachments" on page 79.

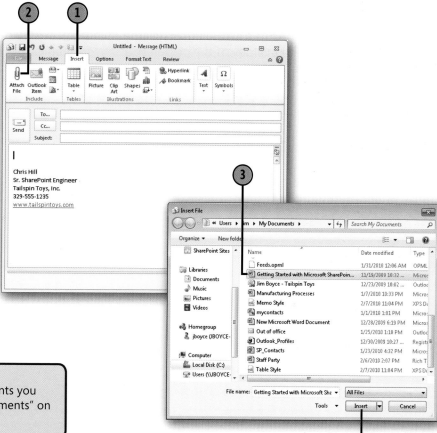

Sending Messages

When you send a message, it travels across the local area network or the Internet to the mailbox of the person you specify as the recipient. If you specify more than one recipient, Outlook sends a copy of the message to everyone you specify. By default, Outlook sends messages automatically as soon as they are placed in the Outbox. You also can configure Outlook to hold your messages in the Outbox until you're ready to send them. (Clicking Send places the message in the Outbox.)

Place a Message in the Outbox

① Create a new message.

② Click Send.

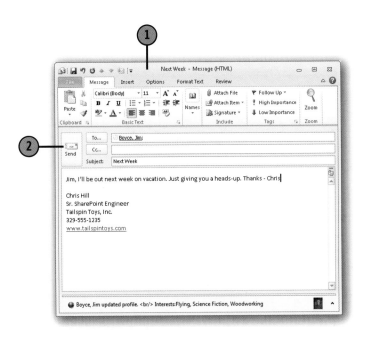

See Also

When you reply to or forward a message, you send it the same way you would send a new mail message. For more information, see "Replying To and Forwarding E-Mail" on page 81.

Caution

If Outlook is set up to send your messages as soon as you click the Send button, you can't change anything in your message before it's routed to your recipients. Even if your message is incomplete or contains confidential information, you can't recall the message (unless you're using Exchange Server).

Transmit E-Mail Messages Manually

(1) In Outlook, click the File tab, Options, and then click Advanced.

(2) Clear the Send Immediately When Connected check box.

(3) Click OK to close the Options dialog box.

(4) Create a new message.

(5) Click Send to send the message to the Outbox folder.

(6) Click Outbox in the Navigation Pane.

(7) Confirm that a message is waiting in the Outbox folder.

(8) To send the message, click the Send/Receive tab on the ribbon and click Send All.

See Also

For information on receiving e-mail messages, see Section 5, "Receiving and Reading E-Mail," starting on page 71.

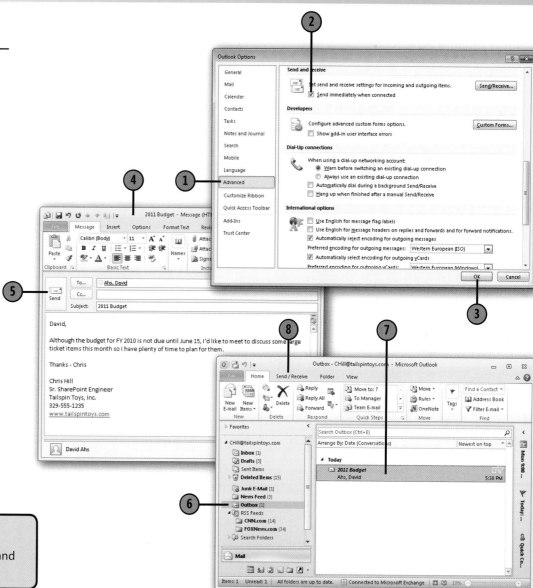

Reviewing Sent Messages and Drafts

When you send a message, Outlook stores a copy of it in the Sent Items folder. This folder enables you to keep track of all the messages you've sent to recipients. You can open this folder and review messages you've sent to other users. Outlook also includes a Drafts folder that stores new messages you're working on but are not ready to send.

Open the Sent Items Folder

① Click the Mail icon on the Navigation Pane.

② Click the Sent Items folder in the Navigation Pane.

③ Review the contents of the Sent Items folder.

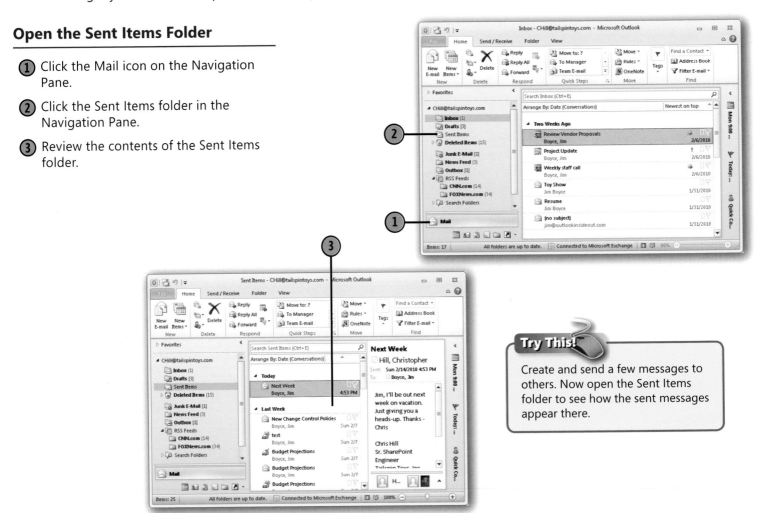

Try This!

Create and send a few messages to others. Now open the Sent Items folder to see how the sent messages appear there.

Open the Drafts Folder

1 Create a new message with recipient, subject, and body text, then click the File tab.

2 Click Save.

3 Click File, and then click Close.

4 Click the Drafts folder in the Navigation Pane.

5 Your saved message is displayed.

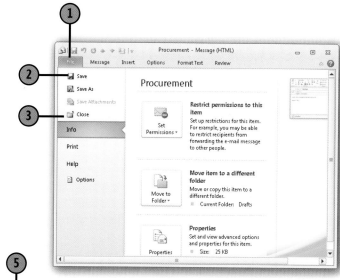

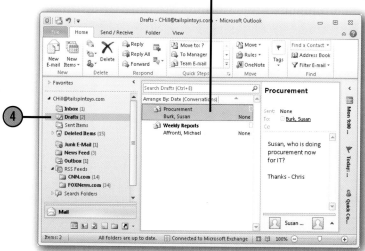

See Also

You can move a message or group of messages from the Drafts folder to the Outbox folder without opening any first. To learn how to move items to different folders, see "Organizing with Folders" on page 215.

5

Receiving and Reading E-Mail

To receive e-mail messages that have been sent to you, Microsoft Outlook 2010 connects to an e-mail server on which messages are stored (such as servers located on a local area network or the Internet) and downloads the messages (or copies of them) to your Inbox folder. From there, you can read a message, reply, forward it to someone, flag it for later action, and open file attachments. In most cases, messages that you download are deleted from the server automatically after they're downloaded.

Outlook can also filter out junk e-mail by blocking mail that contains certain words or phrases or that arrives from certain addresses. You can adjust these filters to block mail from unwanted senders and let through the mail that you want to read. You also can set up Outlook rules, which help you manage your messages by moving them to designated folders, flagging them, or otherwise processing messages in accordance with rules that you define.

This section shows you how to receive, read, reply to, follow up, and forward messages in Outlook. You learn how to manage your Inbox by deleting, saving, and printing messages. Finally, you learn how to handle junk mail, set up rules that personalize your e-mail experience, and work with e-mail attachments.

Receiving E-Mail

Outlook makes it easy for you to receive your incoming messages. You can schedule Outlook to download your new messages, or you can manually download new messages when you want.

Retrieve E-Mail Automatically

1. Click Options on the File tab.
2. Click Advanced.
3. Click Send/Receive.
4. Select the Schedule An Automatic Send/Receive Every *n* Minutes option.
5. Type the number of minutes between each download.
6. Click Close, and then close the Options dialog box.
7. Messages that appear in boldface are ones that you have not read yet.
8. The next time you start Outlook, it downloads any new messages. You can view them by clicking the Inbox folder.

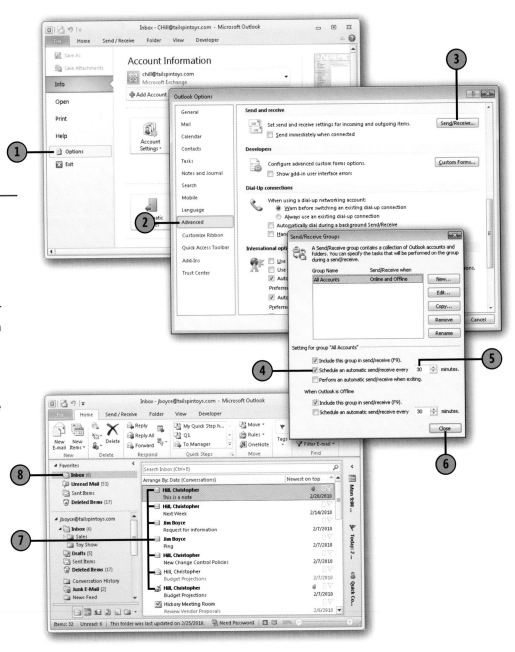

Retrieve E-Mail Manually

① Click Send/Receive All Folders on the Send/Receive tab of the ribbon.

② Click the Inbox icon on the Navigation Pane to see your new messages.

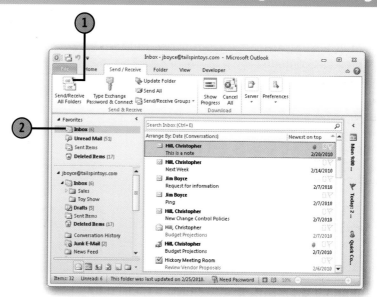

Tip

If you have Outlook configured for several e-mail message services—such as a Microsoft Exchange server and an Internet e-mail service, or two different Internet mail servers—clicking Send/Receive All Folders in the ribbon downloads new messages from all these services. If you want to download messages from only one service, click the Send/Receive Groups button on the Send/Receive tab of the ribbon and then select a service from the Send/Receive Groups menu.

Tip

The total number of e-mail messages in your Inbox folder appears on the status bar, and the number of unread messages appears in the status bar and next to the Inbox icon in the Navigation Pane.

Reading E-Mail

After you receive a message in your Inbox folder, you can preview it or read its contents. The Inbox folder displays the sender's name, the message subject, the date the message was received, the size of the message, and whether the message has an attachment.

Locate New Messages

1 Click the Mail icon on the Navigation Pane to display your new messages.

2 Choose Reading Pane from the View menu, then choose Bottom from the submenu.

3 Click the Received column to sort your new messages by the date you received them. Messages you have not read appear in boldface.

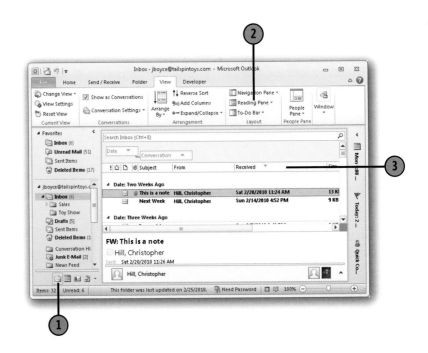

Tip

To find a message from a specific sender, click the From column. This sorts messages alphanumerically based on the sender's name.

Try This!

Click the Received column once. If the most current date is at the top of the list, you're sorting from the most current date received to the earliest date received. Click the Received column again to reverse the order of sorting, from the earliest date to the most current.

Tip

If the Reading Pane is displayed at the right, you can click Newest on Top or Oldest on Top to change the sort order for messages in the Inbox.

Open Message Items

1. Click the Inbox on the Navigation Pane to display your new messages.

2. Click the message you want to read.

3. View its contents in the Reading Pane.

4. Double-click the message to open it.

5. View the message in its own window.

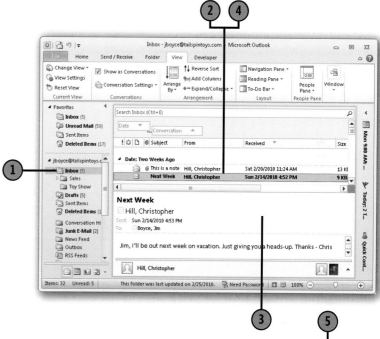

Tip

To turn the Reading Pane off, choose Reading Pane from the View tab, and choose Off from the submenu. To turn it back on, choose Right or Bottom from the Reading Pane menu.

Try This!

You can have Outlook display a few lines of each message by choosing Preview from the Change View button on the View tab of the ribbon. This shows the first few lines of the messages in the Inbox folder.

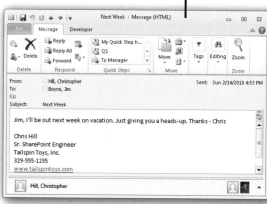

Managing the Inbox Folder

Over time, your Inbox folder can quickly fill with hundreds of messages. This makes finding messages more difficult and takes up hard drive space. You can reduce these problems by managing your Inbox folder. Some of the administrative tasks you can perform include deleting unneeded messages, saving important messages, and printing a copy of a message to read or store in hardcopy format.

Delete Unneeded Messages

1. Click the Inbox icon on the Navigation Pane to display messages in your Inbox folder.

2. Select the message you want to delete.

3. Click Delete on the Home tab of the ribbon.

Caution

Outlook does not ask whether you're sure you want to delete a message. Make sure that you want to delete the message before you press Delete or choose the Delete command. You can press Ctrl+Z to undo a deletion.

Tip

Deleted messages are moved to the Deleted Items folder and can be moved back to your Inbox folder if necessary. If you delete messages from the Deleted Items folder, those items are generally gone for good (unless you copied them to another folder). If you're using Exchange Server, however, you can recover deleted items up to a period of time set by the mail administrator.

See Also

To learn more about managing items and folders, see Section 12, "Managing Items and Folders," starting on page 205.

Save Important Messages

① Click the Inbox icon on the Navigation Pane to display messages in your Inbox folder.

② Select the message you want to save by clicking on it.

③ Click the File tab and choose Save As.

④ If you want to save the message with a different name than the message subject, click in the File Name box and type a new name.

⑤ Choose a folder in which to store the message.

⑥ Click Save.

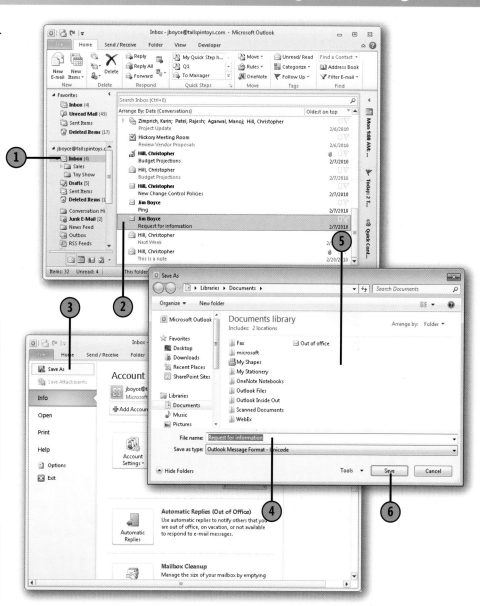

Tip

To save the message in a format other than message format (.msg), click the Save As Type drop-down list and choose the format type. You can save messages in text, HTML, MHT, Outlook template, and two message formats. This makes it handy when you want to open the message in another application, such as a word processor or Internet Web browser. Note that you can't save a plain text message in HTML.

Caution

When you save a message in a format other than .msg, the formatting of the message itself may change. If this is the case, you may find it difficult to read the message without modifying it.

Print a Copy of a Message

① Display or select a message in your Inbox folder.

② Click Print on the File tab.

③ Click the Printer drop-down list, and select the printer you want to use.

④ Click the Print Style option you want.

⑤ Click Print.

Tip

With a message open, click Quick Print from the Quick Access Toolbar to print to the default printer. If Quick Print does not appear on your Quick Access toolbar, you can customize the Quick Access toolbar to add it.

Tip

Use the buttons in the bottom-right corner of the Print page to control print preview options.

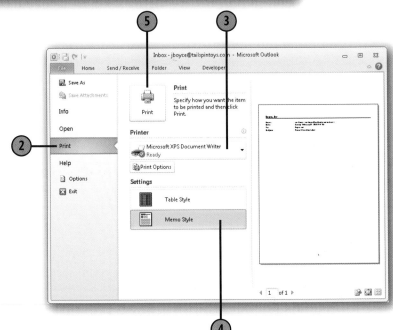

Working with Attachments

When you receive an e-mail attachment, you can open it directly from the message, save it to your hard drive and open it from there, or print it straight from the message to a printer. Messages that have attachments display a paper clip icon to the left of the message author's name or below the message received date, depending on the location of the Reading Pane and the width of the display.

Open an Attachment

① Click the Inbox icon on the Navigation Pane to display messages in your Inbox folder.

② Click the message with the attachment.

③ Double-click the attachment in the Reading Pane.

Tip

To open an attachment, you must have an application that supports the attached file. For example, if you receive a PowerPoint file (.ppt or .pptx), you must have PowerPoint, the PowerPoint Viewer, or some similar application installed on your system to view the file.

See Also

For information on attaching files to messages you send, see "E-Mailing a File" on page 64.

Caution

Some files that you receive from another user, such as programs, Web pages, and script files, can be infected with a computer virus. You should save all executable files to your system and run an antivirus program that checks the file for a virus before you open it. If you receive an attachment from someone you do not know (as happens a lot with junk e-mail), you should never open it. Just delete the message.

Save an Attachment

(1) Click the Inbox icon on the Navigation Pane to display messages in your Inbox folder.

(2) Click the message with the attachment.

(3) Right-click the attachment in the Attachment field.

(4) Choose Save As from the submenu.

(5) Choose the folder where you want to save the file.

(6) Make any necessary changes to the file name. The default file name is the one given by the sender when he or she initially attaches the file to the message.

(7) Click Save.

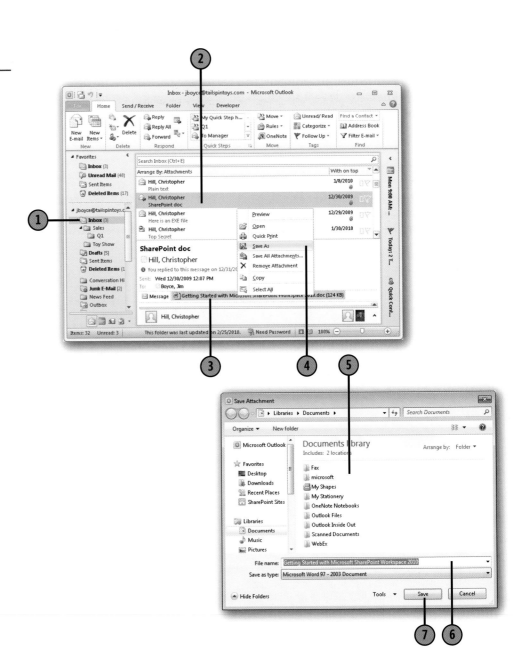

Replying To and Forwarding E-Mail

When you receive a message, you can reply directly to the sender. You can also forward the message or send a response to everyone who receives the message. When you reply to a message, Outlook keeps the original message text and lets you add your new text above the original text. The sender's name becomes the recipient name, and the subject line begins with "RE:" to denote that the message is a reply.

Reply To an E-Mail Message

(1) Click the Inbox icon on the Navigation Pane to display messages in your Inbox folder.

(2) Click the message to which you want to reply.

(3) Click Reply on the Home tab of the ribbon.

(4) Click in the space above the original message line, and type your reply.

(5) Click Send.

Tip

When you reply to messages that have attachments, the reply message does not include the attached file.

Tip

To reply to all recipients of a message, click Reply All on the Home tab of the ribbon.

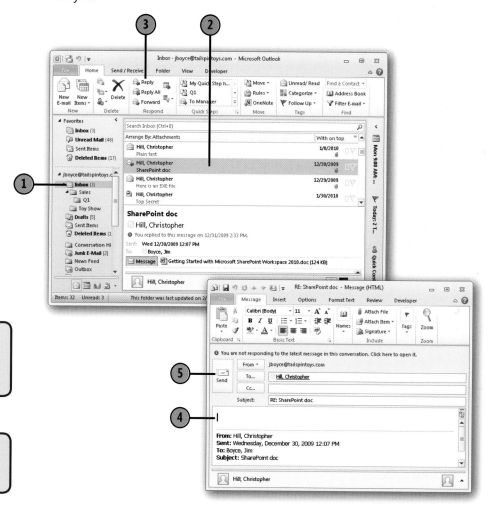

Forward an E-Mail Message

① Click the Inbox icon on the Navigation Pane to display messages in your Inbox folder.

② Click the message you want to forward.

③ Click Forward on the Home tab of the ribbon.

④ Add the address to which you want to forward this message.

⑤ Click in the space above the original message line, and type a message, if you want.

⑥ Click Send.

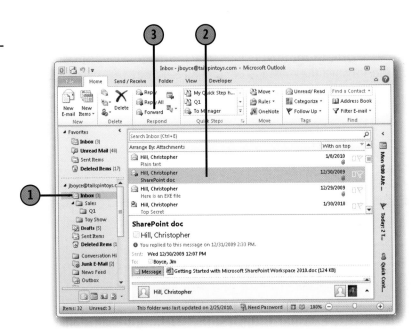

Tip

When you forward messages that have attachments, the forwarded message includes the attached file.

See Also

For information on addressing messages, see "Writing an E-Mail Message" on page 48.

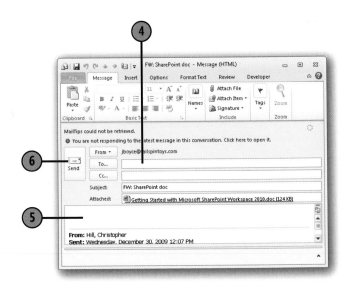

Handling Junk Mail

Just like the junk mail that you receive in your postal mailbox, you probably get too many junk e-mail messages (also known as *spam*) in your Outlook Inbox. Outlook lets you set up mail filters that can sort your incoming mail so that junk mail is moved to its own folder, flagged, or deleted. Outlook also allows you to turn on mail filters so only specific messages are displayed in the Inbox.

Turn On Junk E-Mail Filters

① Click Junk on the Home tab of the ribbon.

② Choose Junk E-mail Options.

③ Choose a junk filtering level.

④ Choose other mail security options as you want.

⑤ Click OK.

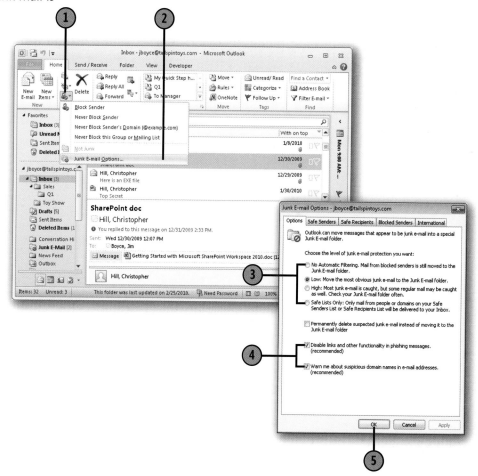

See Also

For more information on setting rules and filters, see "Working with the Rules Wizard" on page 86.

Add to the Junk Mail Senders List

1 In the Inbox folder, click a message from a person who you want to add to the junk mail senders list.

2 Click Junk on the Home tab of the ribbon.

3 Choose Block Sender from the sub-menu. A message box may appear telling you that the sender has been added to the junk e-mail list. Click OK.

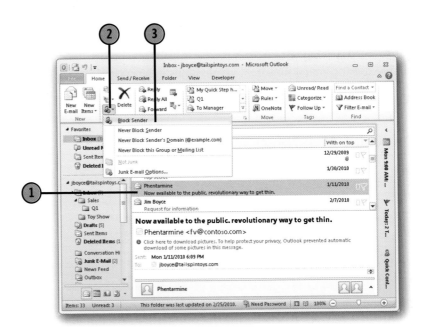

Tip ✓

One way you get on a junk mail list is by filling out surveys and other online forms on Web sites. Usually these forms ask for your e-mail address to process the form. To reduce the amount of junk e-mail you get, limit the number of Web site surveys you fill out or use a "junk" e-mail account you create just for this purpose.

Caution !

If you add a sender to the junk e-mail list by accident, all messages from this sender may be deleted as soon as they're received by Outlook. If you think a legitimate sender has been added to your junk mail filter, see the next procedure for removing him or her from the list.

Fine-Tune the Junk Mail Filter

(1) Click Junk on the Home tab, and then choose Junk E-mail Options.

(2) Click the Blocked Senders tab.

(3) To remove a sender from the Junk Mail list, select a name and click Remove.

(4) To add a sender to the Blocked Senders list, click Add.

(5) Type the e-mail address or domain of the junk mail sender.

(6) Click OK.

(7) Click OK.

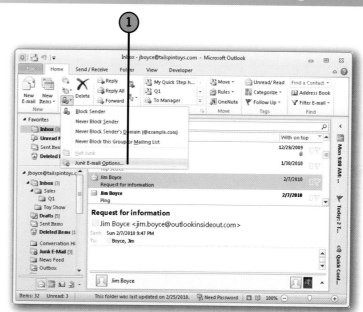

> **Tip**
>
> You can block an entire domain, if needed. Blocking a domain blocks all messages from all addresses in that domain.

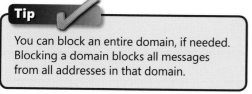

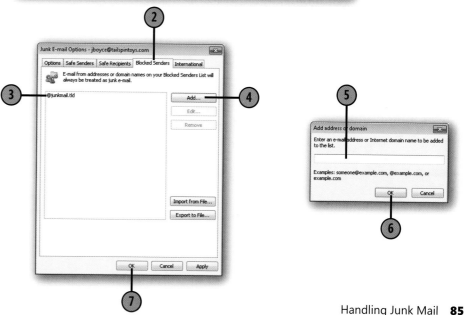

Working with the Rules Wizard

Rules are actions that Outlook performs on your messages to organize them. Once you have Outlook rules set, many management tasks are taken care of automatically when your new messages arrive. To make setting up rules painless, Outlook includes a Rules Wizard that walks you through the process of creating a rule by referring to a message you have already received. You can also create a rule from scratch.

Create a Rule Based on a Message

1. In the Inbox folder, right-click the message on which you want to base the new rule.

2. Click Rules, Create Rule on the shortcut menu to display the Create Rule dialog box.

3. Choose the condition to apply to the rule.

4. Choose the action you want Outlook to perform on messages that match the condition. For example, select the Move The Item To Folder option.

5. Click Select Folder.

6. Choose the folder to which you want the messages moved.

7. Click OK twice.

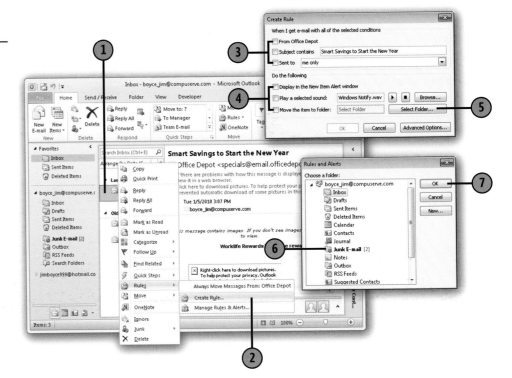

Tip ✓

The conditions and actions available in the Create Rule dialog box are just some of the ones you can use in Outlook. The Rules Wizard, which you access by clicking Rules, Manage Rules And Alerts from the Home tab of the ribbon, offers many additional conditions and actions for message-processing rules.

Tip ✓

You can select multiple conditions under which your new rule is applied. When you do this, however, the rule isn't applied unless all the conditions are met.

Create a Rule from Scratch

① With the Inbox folder displayed, click Rules, and then click Manage Rules & Alerts on the Home tab.

② Click New Rule.

③ Click Apply Rule On Messages I Receive under Start From A Blank Rule.

④ Click Next.

(continued on next page)

Try This!

To run rules manually, click Run Rules Now on the Rules and Alerts dialog box. Select the rules you want to run, and click Run Now.

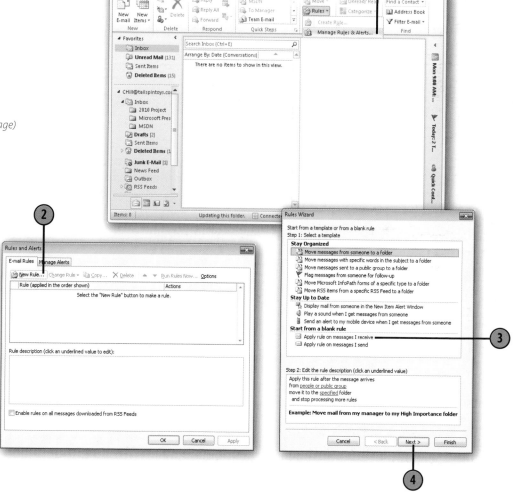

Create a Rule from Scratch *(continued)*

⑤ Select the condition under which you want the rule applied.

⑥ If the condition requires additional configuration, click the link in the Step 2 field and enter the information.

⑦ Click Next.

⑧ Select what you want to do with the message.

⑨ If the action requires further configuration, click the link in the Step 2 field and enter the required information.

⑩ Click Next.

⑪ Select any exceptions to the rule.

⑫ Click Next.

⑬ Type a name for your rule.

⑭ Select Turn On This Rule.

⑮ Click Finish.

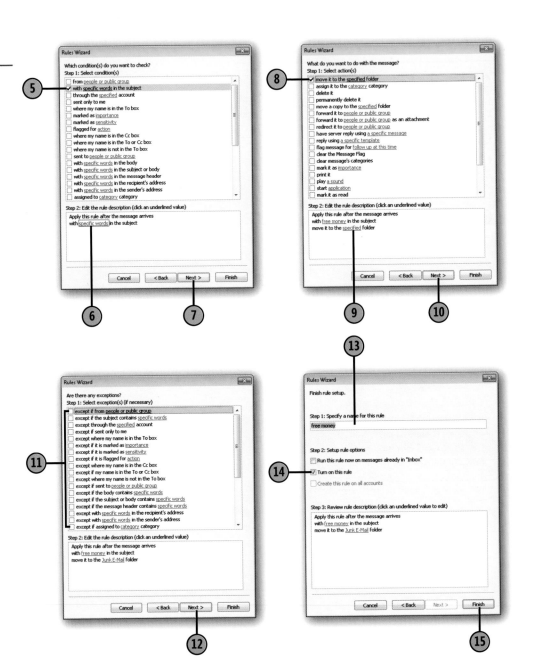

Following Up on a Message

When you receive a message, you may not have time or the information you need to reply to it. In such cases, you can flag a message to remind yourself to follow up on it later. You can designate different types of follow-up, including reminders to reply by e-mail, to forward the message to a third party, or to reply by telephone.

Flag a Message for Follow-Up

① In the Inbox pane, right-click the message you want to return to.

② Choose Follow Up.

③ Select the follow-up action, or click Add Reminder to open the Custom dialog box.

④ Place a check mark in the Reminder check box.

⑤ Select a reminder date.

⑥ Set a time for the reminder, and then click OK.

Try This!

In the Flag For Follow Up dialog box, set a flag that is due today at 30 minutes from the current time. When the time expires, Outlook displays a message prompting you to follow up on the message.

Tip

A small flag appears next to a message you flag.

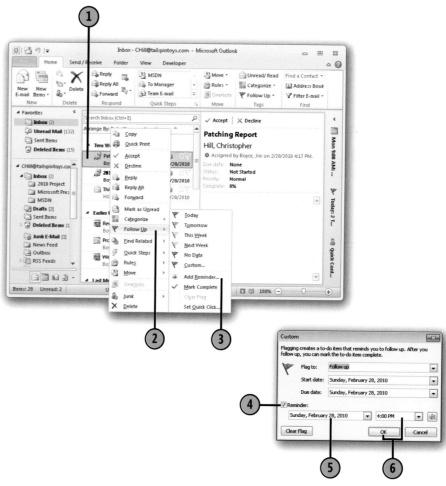

Set Follow-Up Flag Status

① In the Inbox pane, click the follow-up flag to clear or set the flag.

② Or right-click the message and choose Mark Complete.

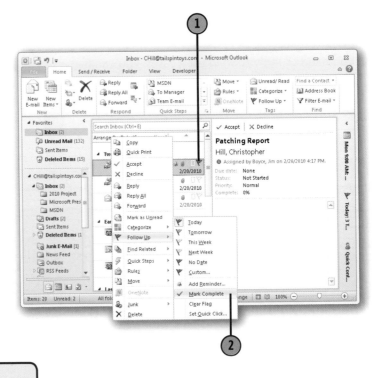

Tip

When you clear a follow-up flag, a clear flag appears next to the message subject. If you later determine that you want to set the flag again, right-click the message, choose Follow Up from the submenu, deselect the Mark Complete option, and click OK.

See Also

For information on replying to e-mail messages, see "Replying To and Forwarding E-Mail" on page 81.

6

Using RSS Feeds in Outlook

Rich Site Summary, now commonly called Really Simple Syndication (RSS), is an XML format that enables simplified publication of news feeds, listings, blogs, and other data. Microsoft Outlook 2010 provides RSS support directly in Outlook, enabling you to subscribe to and read RSS feeds from a variety of sources. For example, you might subscribe to your favorite news site, a sports site, and a blog or two. The data shows up in Outlook, organized neatly into folders. Reading an RSS item is as easy as reading an e-mail message.

Adding and using RSS feeds is very easy. It just takes a few clicks of the mouse to get your favorite information feeds to appear in Outlook. This section explains how to add and manage feeds, view feeds, and manage the folders that store the data in Outlook.

Adding RSS Feeds

When your computer is connected to the Internet, Outlook offers a page of Office-related quick links that you can browse and add, or you can add feeds by typing the URL for the feed.

To view the list of Office feeds, just click the RSS Feeds branch in the Navigation Pane.

Add an RSS Feed Manually

1. Right-click RSS Feeds.
2. Choose Add A New RSS Feed.
3. Type the URL for the RSS feed.
4. Click Add.
5. The feed appears in the Navigation Pane.

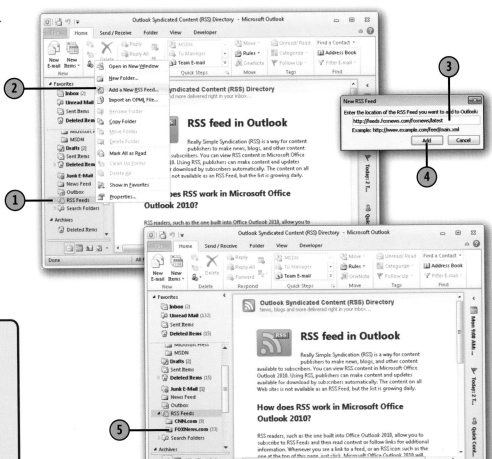

Tip

You don't need to type the URL for each RSS feed you add to Outlook. Instead, find the feed you want to add and highlight the link that points to the feed on the body of the Web page, or navigate to the feed and highlight the link in the browser's Address bar. Then press Ctrl+C to copy the link to the Clipboard. In the New RSS Feed dialog box, press Ctrl+V to paste the RSS link into Outlook.

Viewing RSS Feeds

Because Outlook by default separates your RSS feeds into individual folders, you can easily locate and view content from a specific feed.

(1) In the Outlook Navigation Pane, click to expand the RSS Feeds folder.

(2) Click the feed you want to view.

(3) Look through items to find the one you want to read and then click it.

(4) Preview the item in the Reading Pane.

(5) Click to view the full item in a browser.

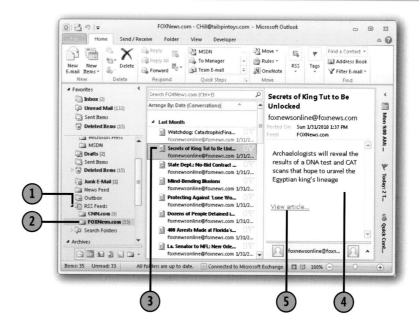

Tip

Click RSS on the Home tab of the ribbon, and choose Download Content, Download Article to download the article to Outlook. The article appears as an HTML attachment to the selected item.

Managing Folders

When you add an RSS feed, Outlook creates a folder to contain the items downloaded from that feed. You can change the name or location of the folder when you add the feed. You can also change the folder name or location at any time after you add the feed, which lets you manage your RSS feeds in a folder structure that suits your needs.

Rename an RSS Folder

1 Click to expand the folder list under RSS Feeds in the Navigation Pane.

2 Right-click the folder and choose Rename Folder, then type a new name and press Enter.

Tip

You can click a folder name to select the folder, and then click it again. Type a new name to rename the folder.

Use a Different Folder
(Change Folder Location)

(1) Click the File tab.

(2) Click Account Settings, and then click Account Settings.

(3) Click the RSS Feeds tab.

(4) Click Change Folder.

(5) Select an existing folder.

(6) Or click New Folder to create a new folder for the feed.

(7) Click OK, then click Close.

Tip

You can move an entire folder to a new location. Just click and drag the folder to its destination.

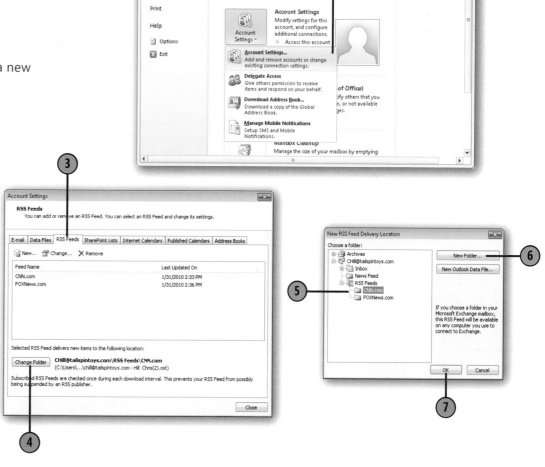

Managing Messages

RSS feed messages are much like e-mail messages you receive in your Inbox. You can mark them as read or unread, delete them, download full article content, move them from one folder to another, and delete the items. You can also easily share a feed with others by sending the feed in an e-mail message. The recipient can then click an icon in the message to add the feed to his or her Outlook RSS subscriptions.

Mark and Unmark RSS Messages

(1) Right-click a message.

(2) Choose Mark As Unread to mark the message as unread. Choose Mark As Read to mark the message as having been read.

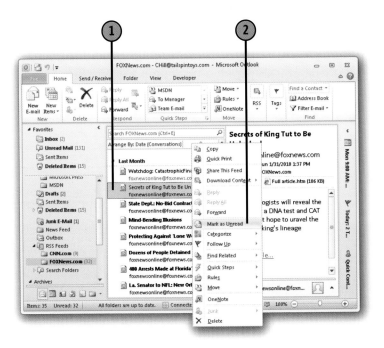

Move Messages Between Folders

① Click the message you want to move.

② Drag the message to the target folder.

③ Or click Move on the Home tab of the ribbon.

④ Select the target folder.

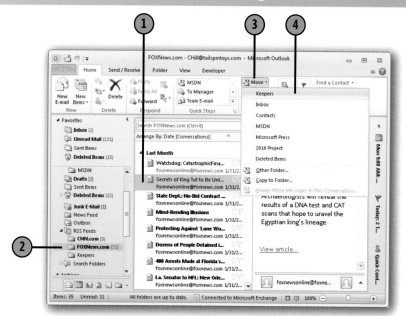

Tip

You can copy a message rather than move it, preserving the message in the original location. To copy a message, press and hold the right mouse button, and then drag the message to the destination and choose Copy from the pop-up menu.

Download a Full Article

① Select a message.

② Click the RSS button on the ribbon.

③ Choose Download Content and then Download Article.

④ After the article has downloaded, double-click the attachment to view the article in your Web browser.

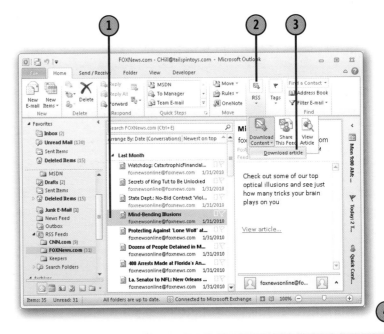

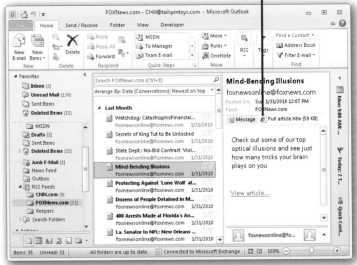

Tip

Downloading an RSS article is useful when you want to keep a copy of the article on your computer. If you're interested only in reading the article but not keeping it, just click the View Article link in the Preview Pane to open the article in your Web browser. Or open the RSS item and click the View Article link in the body of the item to view the article. Reading the article online rather than downloading it saves a little bit of disk space.

7

Working with Contacts

Staying in contact with others is part of life and an important task in business. Whether it's your best friend from high school, a client you've worked with for years, or a new customer, you need a way to store all the information about each one of them.

The Contact feature in Microsoft Outlook 2010 enables you to save personal and business contact information, including phone numbers, addresses, e-mail addresses, Web site information, and personal data. Not merely a glorified card file, the Contacts folder is a full-featured database that lets you use automatic dialing to call a contact, import data from other contact managers or databases (such as Microsoft Access), create new messages to send to a contact, set up contact groups for contacts, and more. Outlook gives you several ways to view your contacts as well. For example, you can view contacts using address cards, group contacts by category, or list them by their phone numbers. As with other folders, Outlook also lets you create custom views.

This section explores the Contacts folder. In it you learn how to create and sort contacts and use them for a variety of tasks. You learn how to send e-mail messages to contacts, work with contacts in your address book, add files to a contact, and organize and manage contacts.

Adding a New Contact

You can add contacts to Outlook's Contacts folder in three ways: by typing new information about someone into a Contacts form, by using information you've entered for another contact, or by using information from an e-mail message. In the latter case, for example, you can quickly create a new contact by using the information from a message that you've received.

Create a Contact from an E-Mail Message

1 With the Inbox showing, select the message that has the contact information you want to save. If you don't have the Reading Pane displayed, open the message to access the From field.

(continued on next page)

Tip

Depending on how the From field is filled out in an e-mail message, you may need to modify the Full Name field when you create a new contact from a mail message. For example, if the sender's name isn't complete or doesn't appear at all, you need to manually enter the information in the address card.

Create a Contact from an E-Mail Message *(continued)*

(2) Right-click the name or address that appears in the From field.

(3) Choose Add To Outlook Contacts from the shortcut menu that appears. A new contact card opens, with some of the new contact's information already entered.

(4) Type the pertinent information into the remaining fields.

(5) Click the Save & Close button to save the contact information.

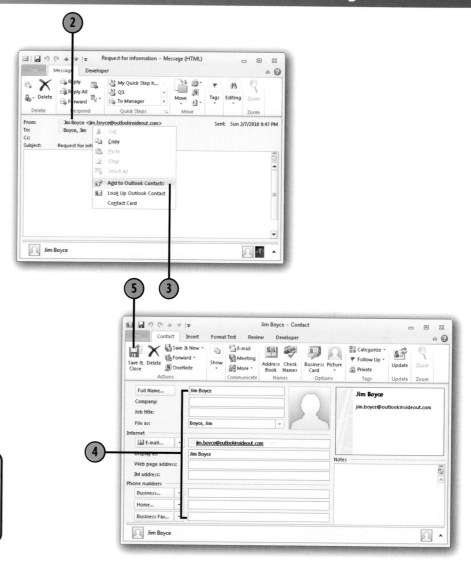

Tip ✓

Click Full Name to open the Check Full Name dialog box. In this box, fill in the complete name and any appropriate prefix (such as "Dr.") or suffix (such as "Jr."). Click OK.

Use the Contact Window

① Click the Contacts icon on the Navigation Pane to display the Contacts folder.

② Click New Contact.

③ Type information about your contact in the appropriate fields.

④ From the File As drop-down list, select one of the ways in which Outlook can display the contact's name, such as last name first, first name last, and so on.

⑤ Type any additional useful information in the Notes box at the bottom of the address card.

⑥ Click Save & Close to save your changes.

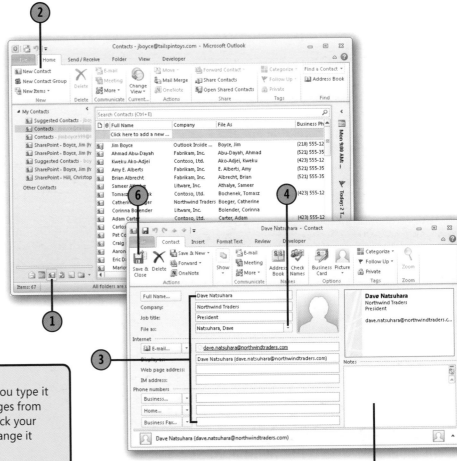

Caution

When you type a contact's e-mail address, be sure you type it correctly. An incorrect address prevents your messages from being sent successfully. Take the time to double-check your spelling of an e-mail address. You can, of course, change it later, but it's best to make sure it's correct now.

Tip

If the contact already exists in your Contacts folder, Outlook asks whether you want to update the information in the existing contact with the new information.

Tip

If you want to keep the Inbox open and also open Contacts, right-click Contacts on the Navigation Pane and choose Open in New Window.

Tip

To make sure that Outlook can dial the phone number for a contact, type phone numbers as numbers; don't use acronyms or letters.

Inserting Items into a Contact Record

You can add Outlook items, application and document objects, and files to a contact by using the Outlook Item button on the Insert tab of the ribbon. For example, you can add an e-mail message to a contact for future reference, insert an attachment, or insert a Microsoft Excel worksheet. You can then access these items from the contact card. You can add a new, empty item and then modify it right in the Outlook item, or you can insert an existing document.

Add an Outlook Item

(1) In an open contact, click in the Notes box.

(2) Click the Insert tab on the ribbon.

(3) Click Outlook Item.

(4) Click the Outlook folder in which the item you want to insert is located.

(5) Select an item in the Items list.

(6) Select the format of the item: Text Only, Attachment, or Shortcut.

(7) Click OK to insert the item into the contact item.

(8) The item now appears with the contact.

(9) Click the Contact tab on the ribbon, and click Save & Close.

See Also

For more information about Outlook items, see "Working with Outlook Items" on page 34.

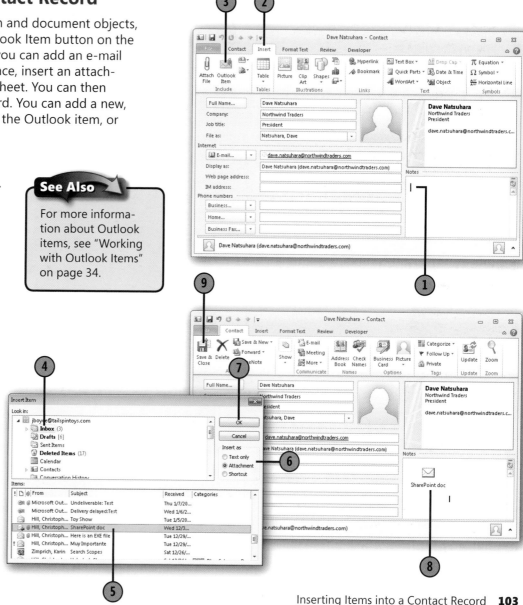

Add a File

① Open a contact, and click the Insert tab on the ribbon.

② Click the Attach File button.

③ Select the folder in which the file you want to insert is located.

④ Select the file you want to insert.

⑤ Click Insert.

⑥ The file now appears with the contact.

⑦ Click the Contact tab on the ribbon, and click Save & Close.

Try This!

To remove a file from a contact, click the file and press Delete.

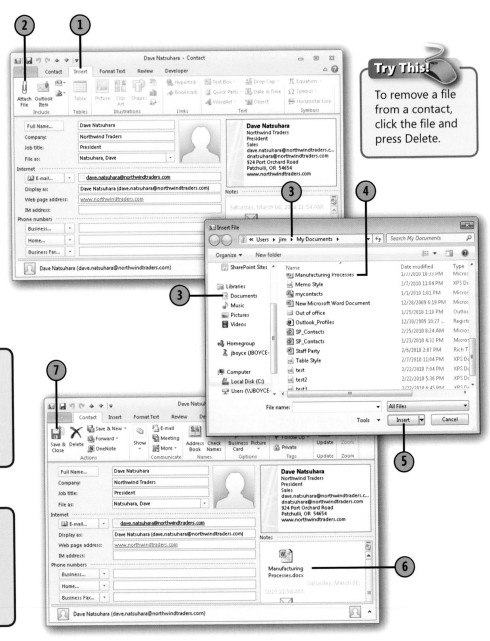

Tip

After you insert a file into a contact's card, you can open it to view, edit, or print it. To do this, double-click the file's icon in the contact item to launch the file within its associated application. Note that this edits the file embedded in the contact, not the original file on disk.

Caution

As you add items, files, and objects to a contact, the size of that contact card increases. When you add several items, files, or objects to a contact, it takes longer for Outlook to open the contact. You should limit the number of attachments you add to a contact.

Viewing Your Contacts Folder

Outlook lets you view your contacts as a series of single address cards or all at once, moving through your Contacts folder as if it were an electronic phone book or address book.

Another way to look at your contact information is through the Outlook Address Book, which lists contacts alphabetically.

Use the Contacts Folder

1. Click the Contacts icon on the Navigation Pane.

2. Click the View tab on the ribbon.

3. Click Change View.

4. Select the view type you want to use to view the contact information in the Contacts folder. You can choose from the following list:

   • Business Card

   • Card

   • Phone

   • List

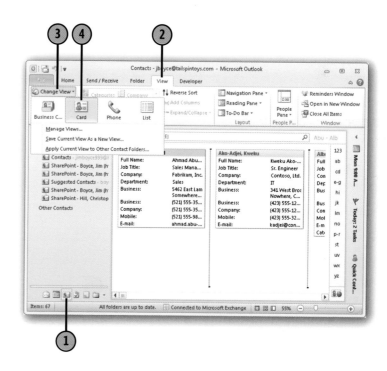

See Also

One task that no one wants to face is typing in all their contacts a second time. This is why it's a good idea to set up a backup schedule to make sure your contacts are backed up at least once a week. For information on backing up and restoring Outlook Contacts, see "Backing Up and Restoring a Data File" on page 230.

Try This!

To see how Outlook displays your contact information in different formats, select each of the views in the Change View drop-down list. When you see one that you like, such as the Phone view, keep it so that the next time you open the Contacts folder that view is showing.

Add a Contact in the Address Book

1. Click Address Book on the Home tab of the ribbon.

2. Choose New Entry from the File menu.

3. Click New Contact in the New Entry dialog box.

4. Choose a location for the new contact.

5. Click OK.

6. Add the new contact information to the appropriate fields.

7. Click Save & Close.

See Also

For more information on using and modifying contact information via the Address Book, see "Working with the Address Book" on page 50.

Tip

You can add contact groups to the Contacts folder using the Address Book. Rather than clicking New Contact in the Select The Entry Type dialog box, click New Contact Group. The new contact group appears in the Contacts folder alongside individual entries.

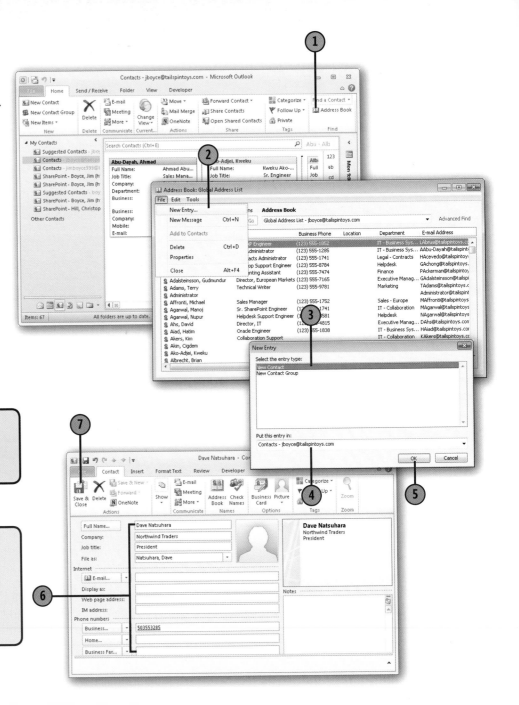

Viewing Contact Information

After you create a contact, you can view it in the Contacts folder or open it in its own address card. In the Contacts folder, you can see the contact's name, company, title, selected phone information, e-mail address, and postal address. To see a contact's full set of information, you must display the contact form. When you view the contact, you can print the information, view activities associated with a contact, and display a map to the address.

Print Contact Information

① Click the Contacts icon in the Navigation Pane.

② Double-click the contact you want to print.

(continued on next page)

Tip

To print attachments inserted into a contact, first open the contact and choose Print from the File tab. Click Print Options and select Print Attached Files in the Print dialog box. The attachments open in their associated application (for example, an Excel worksheet opens in Excel) and print. The attachments print to the default printer, even if you select a different printer in the Outlook Print dialog box.

Print Contact Information *(continued)*

③ Click the File tab.

④ Click Print.

⑤ Verify options in the Print dialog box, and click Print.

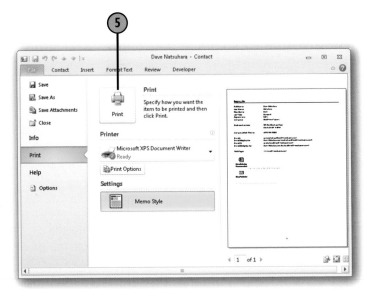

Use the Activities Tab

① Click the Contacts icon on the Navigation Pane.

② Double-click the contact name you want to view.

③ In the ribbon, click Show.

④ Click Activities.

⑤ Click the Show drop-down list and select the type of item you want to view.

⑥ Double-click an item to open it.

Tip ✓

Searching for activities associated with a contact can take a long time if the contact has a long list of items associated with it. If it takes too long, you can stop the search at any time by clicking the Stop button on the right side of the Activities tab.

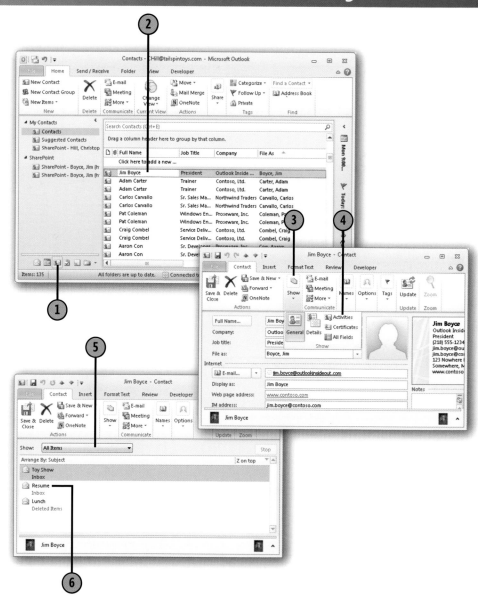

Display a Map

① Click the Contacts icon on the Navigation Pane.

② Double-click the contact for which you want to display a map.

③ On the Contact tab of the ribbon, in the Communicate group, click More, Map It. Or click the Map It button to the right of the address field on the contact form.

④ View the map in your Web browser.

Tip

To see a map for an address, you must have Internet access.

Caution

Not all addresses are available from the Bing Web site. If you can't find the address you're looking for, modify the information you enter on the search Web page. Click the Search button to begin the search again.

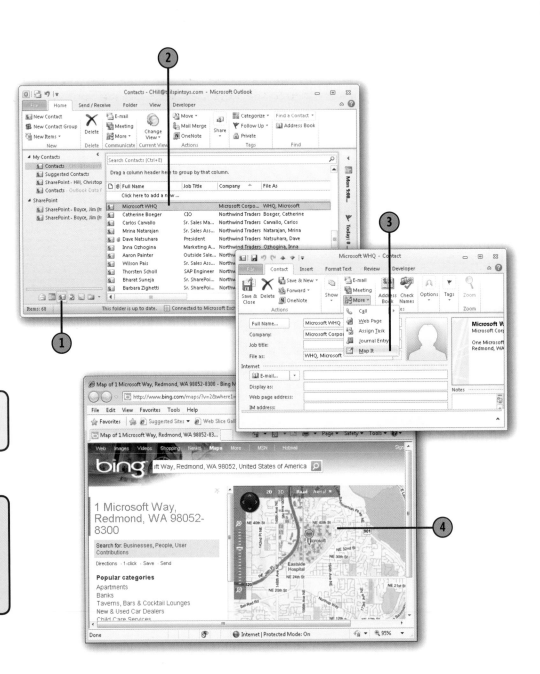

Updating an Existing Contact

You can store a lot of information about a person or company in a single address item. For many contacts, however, you're likely to start by typing only the most critical information. You might find later that you need to update the information.

It's easy to do: simply open the Contacts folder, locate the contact you want to update, open the contact item for that person, and make your changes.

Use the Contacts Folder

1. Click the Contacts icon on the Navigation Pane.

2. Select the View tab on the ribbon, and then select a view from the Change View button.

3. Click in the scroll bar to navigate through the list of contacts.

4. Double-click a contact to open its form for viewing or modification.

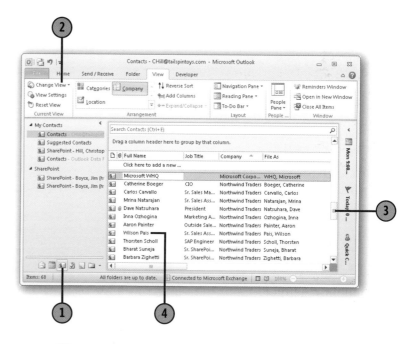

See Also

For information on using contacts in e-mail messages, see Section 4, "Writing and Sending E-Mail," starting on page 47.

Tip ✓

When you view contacts using the Business Card or Address Cards, you can click the letter buttons on the right side of the window to jump to contacts whose names start with that letter. For example, click the letter *m* to jump to contacts named *Mitchell, Mosley,* and so on.

Finding a Contact

You can search for contacts in Outlook by using Instant Search or the Find A Contact box—or simply by scrolling through the list of your contacts. You don't even have to know the complete name of the person you are looking for in Outlook because searching for part of a name brings up any name that matches that string.

Scroll Through the Contacts Folder

① Click the Contacts icon on the Navigation Pane.

② Select the View tab, click Change View, and then select Card from the sub-menu. (You can also use the Business Card view.)

③ Move the scroll bar at the bottom of the Contacts folder to scroll through your contacts.

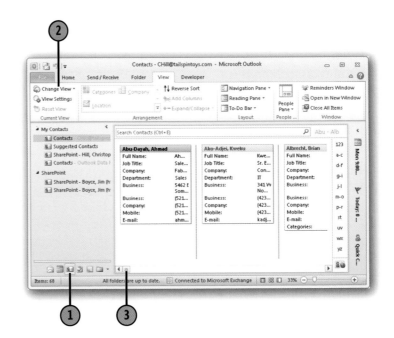

Caution

Be careful when you view contacts in the Contacts folder. If you press Delete after clicking on a contact, you delete the contact. If this happens, press Ctrl+Z to undo the deletion.

Tip

If your Contacts folder is really large, scrolling through the list of contacts isn't the most efficient way to locate a contact. Instead, use the Find A Contact box or Instant Search to locate the contact.

Use Instant Search

① Click the Contacts icon on the Navigation Pane.

② Click in the Search box.

③ Type the name of the contact you want to find.

④ Double-click the contact to open it.

⑤ Click either X to clear the search.

See Also

For information on finding names in the Address Book, see "Find a Name in the Address Book" on page 51.

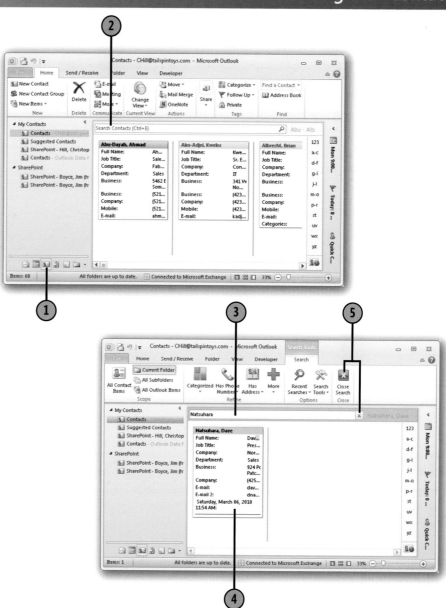

Use the Advanced Find Dialog Box

① Click the Contacts icon on the Navigation Pane.

② Click in the Search box to display the Search Tools on the ribbon.

③ Click Search Tools, and then Advanced Find.

④ Type a word or phrase in the Search For The Word(s) field.

⑤ Select the fields in which to search.

⑥ Click Find Now to search for contacts matching the search criteria.

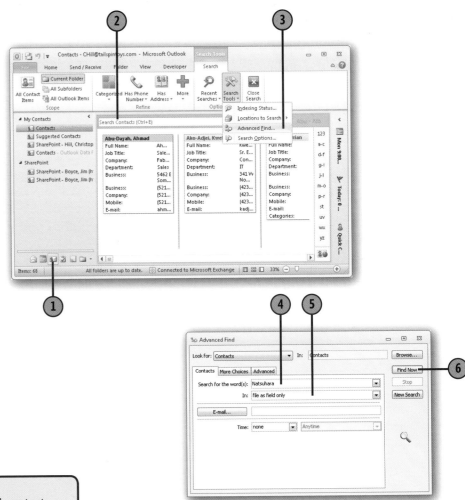

Tip

You can use the Advanced Find dialog box to find contacts using a number of search criteria. For example, you can search for contacts who have a specific e-mail address or domain name in the e-mail address. This is handy if you know that a contact has a domain name of @tailspintoys.com but aren't sure of her name or complete e-mail address. Simply type **@tailspintoys.com** in the E-mail field, and press Enter.

Tip

Click New Search to clear your search results so you can begin a new one. Click OK when the prompt tells you that beginning a new search loses the results of the previous search.

Organizing Your Contacts

When you have only a few dozen or so contacts, finding and managing them is fairly easy. You can simply open the Contacts folder, scroll through the list, and find what you're looking for. However, after the Contacts folder grows, you need to organize your contacts to make them easier to find and update.

Outlook gives you three ways to organize your contacts. You can use folders to store related contacts, use categories to set up relationships between contacts, or use views to sort contacts in ways that make sense to you.

Use Folders

① Click the Contacts icon on the Navigation Pane.

② Click the Folder tab.

③ Click New Folder.

(continued on next page)

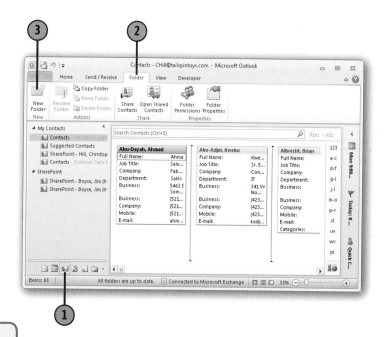

Try This!

After you create a folder for contacts, you can drag existing contacts to your new folder to organize them as necessary. For example, create a folder named "Project Team" in the Contacts folder. Open the Folder List in the Navigation Pane so that you can see the new folder, but keep the focus on the Contacts folder. Drag members from your project team into the Project Team folder. You now can quickly see who is on your team by clicking this folder.

Use Folders *(continued)*

④ Type a name for the folder in the Name field.

⑤ Click the Folder Contains drop-down list, and select Contact Items.

⑥ Click OK.

⑦ Click the folder in the Navigation Pane to view the new folder.

Caution

When you create a new folder for contacts, make sure the Contact Items option is selected in the Folder Contains drop-down list.

Tip

Your new contacts folder appears in the My Contacts area of the Navigation Pane when you're in Contacts. You don't have to open the Folder List to access the additional contacts folders.

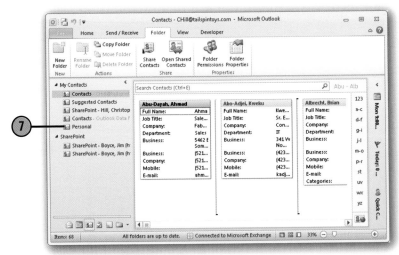

Use Categories

1 Click the Contacts icon on the Navigation Pane.

2 Right-click a contact, and select Categorize from the shortcut menu.

3 Select the category to which you want the contact to belong.

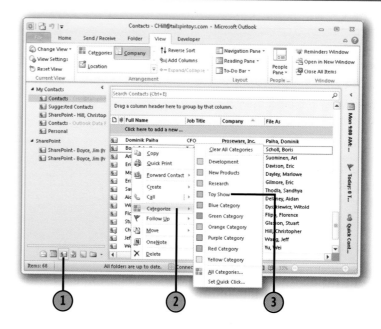

Tip

You can add your own categories and modify existing ones. Choose Categorize from the Tags group on the Home tab, and then choose All Categories to open the Color Categories dialog box, where you can add and modify categories.

See Also

For more information on Outlook Categories, see "Using Categories" on page 206.

Customize Views

① Click the Contacts icon on the Navigation Pane, and then display the view you want to customize.

② Click the View tab, and then click View Settings.

③ Click Columns to open the Show Columns dialog box.

④ Click a column in the Available Columns list.

⑤ Click Add to add the field to the view.

⑥ Click a field you want to remove.

⑦ Click Remove.

⑧ Click OK.

⑨ Click Other Settings.

(continued on next page)

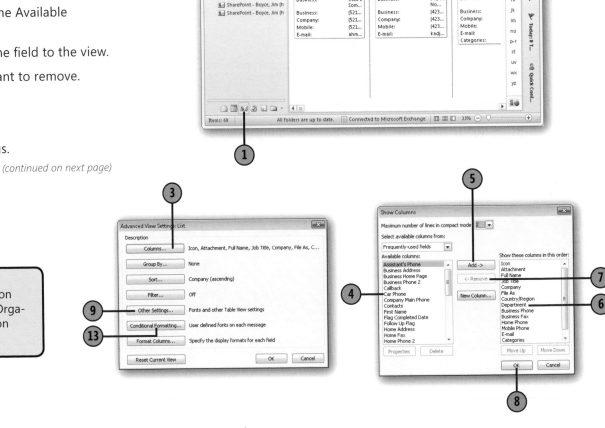

See Also

For more information on sorting contacts, see "Organizing Your Contacts" on page 115.

Customize Views *(continued)*

10 Use the Font buttons to choose a font for Card Headings and Card Fields.

11 Enter the card dimensions you want in Card Width And Multi-Line Field Height.

12 Click OK.

13 Click Conditional Formatting.

14 Click Add.

15 Type a name for the new rule.

16 Click Condition.

17 Enter your search conditions for the rule.

18 Click OK.

19 Click Font and choose a font for the new rule, and then click OK.

20 Click OK, and then click OK to close the Advanced View Settings dialog box.

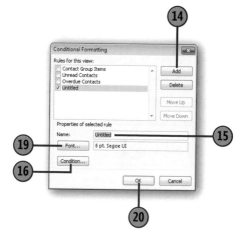

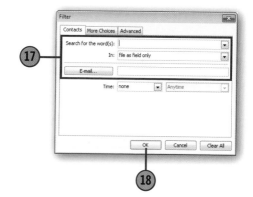

Try This!

Create a customized view by selecting Customize Current View from the Current View submenu. Click Filter, and specify the filtering criteria for your custom view. For example, if you want Outlook to show only those contacts that have a specific e-mail domain name, type that domain name in the E-mail field.

Tip

You can create and use customized views in any Outlook folder, not just the Contacts folder.

Communicating with Contacts

Microsoft Outlook makes it easy to communicate with your contacts. You can open the Contacts folder and create a new e-mail message while viewing a contact's address card, or you can use Outlook's phone dialing feature to call a contact.

E-Mail a Contact

1. Click the Contacts icon on the Navigation Pane.
2. Click a contact.
3. Click E-mail on the Home tab of the ribbon.
4. Type a subject in the Subject field.
5. Type your message.
6. Click Send.

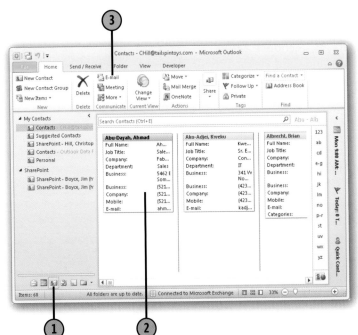

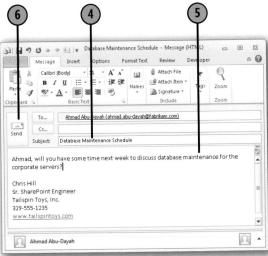

Tip

To send a message to multiple contacts, press Ctrl as you click contact names in the Contact folder. Then click E-mail on the Home tab to open a new message for those contacts.

Caution

If you select a contact that doesn't have an e-mail address, you receive an error message that tells you the selected contact doesn't have an e-mail address or that another problem exists. You can click OK to continue, but you can't send the message to that contact until you provide a valid e-mail address.

Telephone a Contact

① Click the Contacts icon on the Navigation Pane.

② Click the contact you want to call.

③ Click More on the Home tab.

④ Place the pointer over Call.

⑤ Choose the number to call.

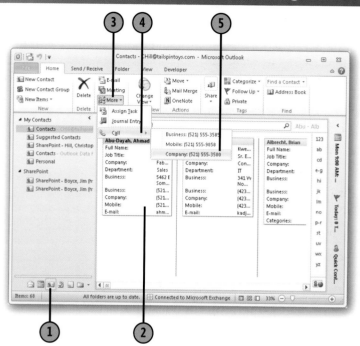

Tip

You can track the amount of time spent on a call with the Outlook Journal. This is handy if you need to track call information, including who you call, when you make the call, and the length of time the call takes.

Tip

If you don't have a Voice over Internet Protocol (VoIP) phone or voice conferencing application such as Office Communicator, you must have a telephone or headset connected to your modem (or the modem and phone must share the same line) for the AutoDialer option to work.

Scheduling Meetings and Tasks for a Contact

The Contacts folder provides tools to let you schedule meetings and assign tasks to contacts. Meetings are appointments to which you invite others and for which you schedule resources, such as meeting rooms and overhead projectors. You can select the contacts that you want to invite to a meeting and then let Outlook send messages that invite them to the meeting. You also can set up appointments with a contact in the same way, including recurring appointments that occur at the same time every day, week, month, or quarter.

Request a Meeting with a Contact

1 Click the Contacts icon in the Navigation Pane.

2 Click the contact to whom you want to send a meeting request.

3 Click Meeting on the Home tab.

(continued on next page)

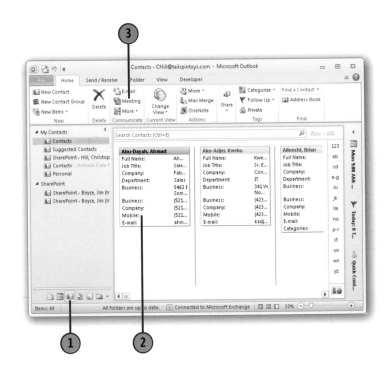

See Also

For information on managing your calendar, including appointments, see Section 8, "Managing a Calendar," starting on page 125.

Tip

Setting up meetings and appointments for contacts works best in conjunction with Microsoft Exchange Server, but you can also use the process with non-Exchange accounts.

Request a Meeting with a Contact *(continued)*

④ Type the subject of the meeting in the Subject field in the Meeting window.

⑤ Select or type a location in the Location drop-down list.

⑥ Type information about the meeting in the meeting body area.

⑦ Choose a start time.

⑧ Choose an end time.

⑨ Click Send.

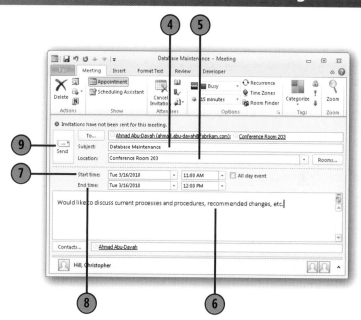

Tip

To set up a schedule for a recurring meeting, click the Recurrence button in the Options group on the Meeting window. Select the meeting time, how often the meeting should recur, and the recurrence pattern (such as "every Friday at 8 AM").

Try This!

You can set meeting reminders using the Meeting window. Select Reminder and choose a time you want the reminder to display. Click the sound icon to pick a sound file that plays when the reminder is activated.

Sharing Contact Information

As you build your contact list, you may want to share it with others in your company or among your circle of friends. Outlook enables you to share contact information by forwarding it as an Outlook Contact item or *vCard*. The vCard format is a standard that several e-mail clients other than Outlook support, enabling you to share contacts with others who might not have Outlook.

Forward a Contact Item

1. Right-click the Contacts icon in the Navigation Pane.

2. Click the contact you want to share.

3. Choose Forward Contact, and then choose either As A Business Card or As An Outlook Contact.

4. Add an e-mail address to the message.

5. Type a message in the message body area.

6. Click Send.

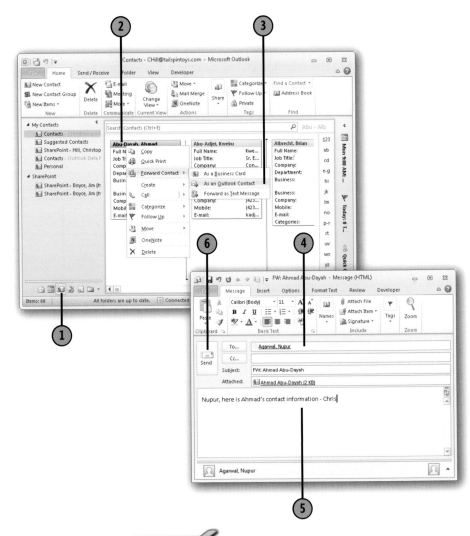

See Also

For information on importing items into Outlook, see "Importing and Exporting Items" on page 226.

Tip ✓

When the recipient receives the forwarded contact item, he or she can import the information into Outlook.

8

Managing a Calendar

The Microsoft Outlook 2010 calendar simplifies the burden of keeping and maintaining a schedule of meetings, appointments, events, and tasks. At a glance, you can quickly see your agenda in daily, weekly, or monthly views. With Outlook, you won't have any excuses for missing a lunch date or forgetting a meeting.

Outlook enables you to keep track of recurring meetings or events so that you don't have to manually enter these items each time they take place. For example, you might have a weekly staff meeting that takes place every Friday from 9:00 A.M. to 10:00 A.M. Make it a recurring meeting, and Outlook blocks out that day and time. Similarly, if your PTA meets every third Tuesday of the month at 7:00 P.M., you can set Outlook to schedule that meeting as well.

Outlook includes an alert that displays a message prior to your Calendar meeting, appointment, or task so that you won't forget it. For example, you can set up Outlook to display a reminder of an upcoming meeting two or three days before its occurrence. If you need to prepare a presentation, document, or other item for the meeting, you give yourself ample time to do so. You then can "snooze" the reminder so it gets your attention again later, but perhaps only three hours prior to the meeting.

Viewing Your Calendar

You can view your Outlook calendar in several different formats. Day view is an hour-by-hour view of your daily schedule, whereas Month view shows your schedule for the entire month. The Date Navigator is a small calendar with which you can navigate quickly to a specific day, week, or month, while the To-Do Bar consolidates all of the features of task list, Date Navigator, and appointment list into one task pane.

Use the Date Navigator

① Click the Calendar icon on the Navigation Pane.

② Click the Day button on the Home tab.

③ Click a day on the Date Navigator to display it in the Calendar view.

④ Click to the left of a week on the Date Navigator to display that week in the Calendar view.

⑤ Click the right arrow on the Date Navigator to move to the next month.

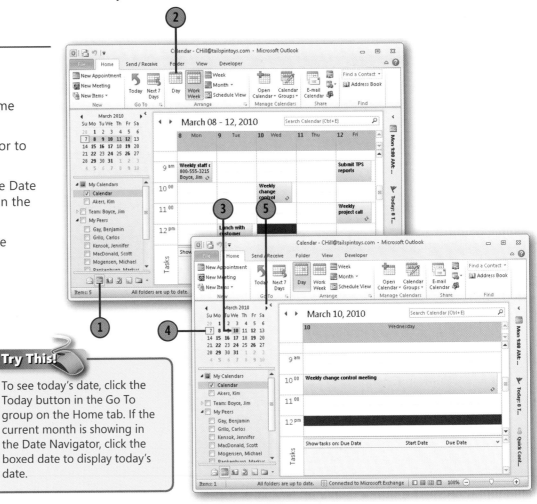

Tip

You can access the current, last three, and next three months by clicking the month name in the Date Navigator. This is handy if you want to jump back a few months or jump forward a month or two.

Try This!

To see today's date, click the Today button in the Go To group on the Home tab. If the current month is showing in the Date Navigator, click the boxed date to display today's date.

Use the Calendar View

1. Click the Calendar icon on the Navigation Pane.

2. Click to see an hourly breakdown of your day.

3. Click Work Week to see a workweek's schedule by hour.

4. Click Week to see a week's scheduling (including weekend days).

5. Click Month to see a month's schedule.

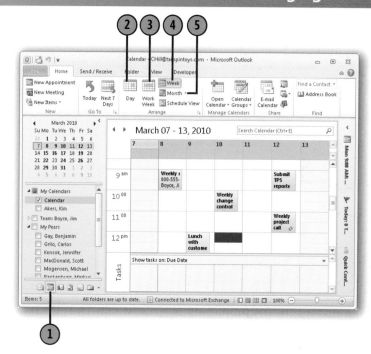

Tip
You can make more room available for the Calendar pane on the screen by resizing or minimizing the Navigation Pane.

Tip
To return to today's date, right-click inside a view and choose Today from the shortcut menu that appears.

Use the To-Do Bar

 Click the Calendar icon on the Navigation Pane.

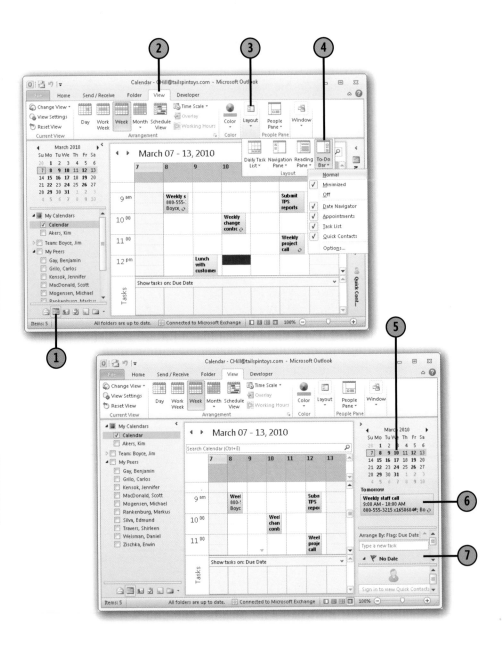 Click the View tab.

③ Click Layout.

④ Click To-Do Bar, and then choose Normal.

Tip

Choose the Minimized option from the To-Do Bar submenu to make the To-Do Bar automatically hide at the edge of the Outlook window.

⑤ Click a date on the Date Navigator to view appointments for that date.

⑥ View upcoming appointments.

⑦ View current tasks.

Tip

Depending on the options you set for the To-Do Bar, portions of the Appointments or Tasks areas of the To-Do Bar might be blank.

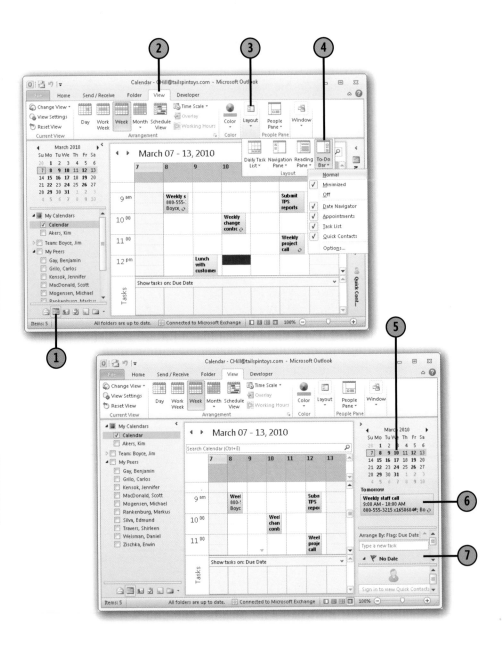

Adding an Appointment

An appointment in Outlook is an activity you enter for a specific time that, unlike a meeting, doesn't typically involve other people or resources. When you schedule an appointment, you block out a day, a time, and a location for that appointment to occur. As mentioned earlier, Outlook also lets you set a reminder that flashes on your screen and plays a sound to alert you to the appointment. To learn how to set a reminder, see the task "Working with Reminders" on page 144.

Add an Appointment with the Menu

1. Click the Calendar icon on the Navigation Pane.

2. Select a block of time for the appointment.

3. Click New Appointment on the Home tab.

(continued on next page)

Tip

Keep your appointment subjects as short as possible so that they're easy to read in the Calendar view.

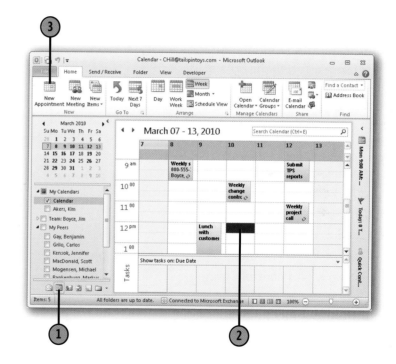

Add an Appointment with the Menu *(continued)*

④ Type a description of the appointment in the Subject box.

⑤ Type the location of the appointment in the Location box.

⑥ Click the down arrow to the right of the Start Time date, and select the day of the appointment.

⑦ Click the down arrow to the right of the Start Time hour, and select the starting time of the appointment.

⑧ Click the down arrow to the right of the End Time date, and select the ending day of the appointment if the appointment spans multiple days.

⑨ Click the down arrow to the right of the End Time hour, and select the ending time of the appointment.

⑩ Add notes if you want.

⑪ Click the Save & Close button.

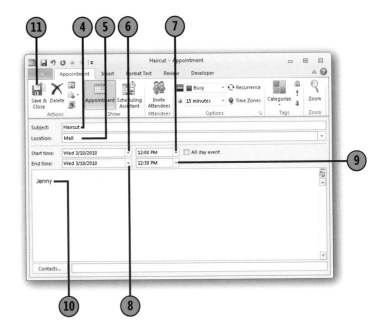

Try This!

If you'd like to add extended information about an appointment, click in the text area at the bottom of the Appointment window. Type a longer description here, such as directions to the appointment location, important information about the appointment, and so on.

Tip

You can print your appointments to the default printer by clicking the Print button on the File tab.

Add an Appointment Right on the Calendar

① Click the Calendar icon on the Navigation pane.

② Click and drag to select a block of time for the appointment on the Calendar.

③ Begin typing the Subject of the appointment, and the subject appears in the blocked-out space on the Calendar.

④ Press Enter.

⑤ Double-click the appointment to open the appointment form.

⑥ Add the location, notes, and other information to the appointment.

⑦ Click the Save & Close button.

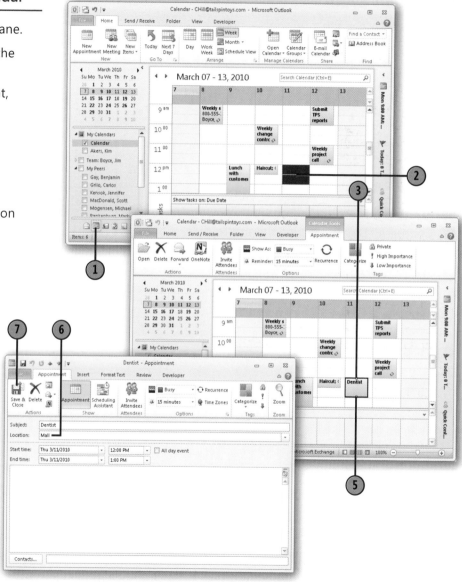

Tip

If you use Outlook with a Microsoft Exchange Server account, others can easily see your free/busy time. They know when you're busy and can schedule meetings with you based on this information.

Tip

To categorize the appointment, right-click the appointment and choose Categorize, and then choose a category from the submenu.

Adding an Event

An event is an activity that runs for 24 hours or longer. An example of an event is a weeklong conference or seminar that you attend. Events display as banners at the top of the day and run from midnight to midnight, so they don't take up blocks of time on the Calendar. This display method leaves room in your calendar for you to show appointments or meetings that you might schedule during event days.

Describe the Event

① Click the Calendar icon on the Navigation Pane.

② Click a day on the calendar.

③ Click the New Items button.

④ Choose All Day Event from the short-cut menu.

⑤ Type a description of the event in the Subject box.

⑥ Type the location of the event in the Location box.

⑦ Click the Save & Close button.

Tip

To add an all-day event to a day other than the current day, display the week or month, right-click on the day, and then choose New All Day Event.

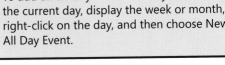
Try This!

You can add more information about an event to the text area at the bottom of the Event window.

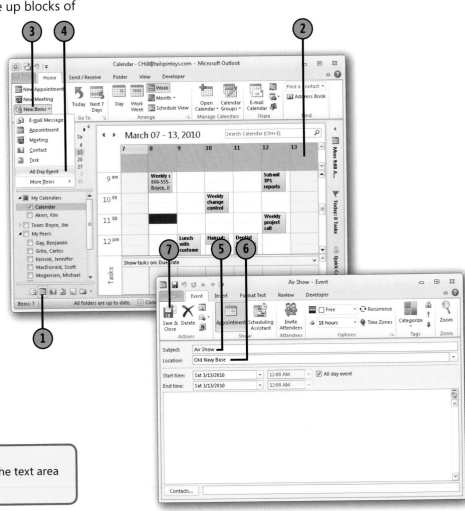

Change the Event's Scheduled Date

(1) Create a new event.

(2) Add a subject and location for the event.

(3) Click the Start Time date down arrow and select the starting day of the event.

(4) Click the End Time date down arrow and select the ending day of the event if it is a multiple-day event.

(5) Click the Save & Close button.

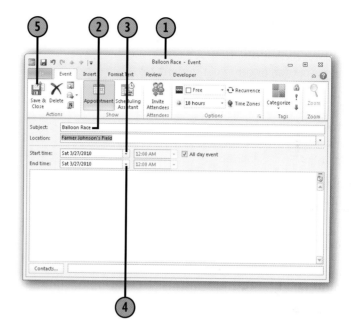

 Tip

You may already have events entered in your Calendar folder. When you create a new contact in the Contacts folder and include a birthday or anniversary for the contact, Outlook schedules that date as an event in the calendar.

 See Also

For information on setting up contacts, see Section 7, "Working with Contacts," starting on page 99.

Setting Up a Meeting

A meeting is an activity (often a physical meeting or conference call) that involves other people and sometimes resources. A resource can be a conference room, VCR, slide projector, telephones, laptop computer, or other equipment. Usually a meeting involves you and at least two other people (but can certainly be just you and one other person). Outlook sends a meeting invitation to every person you designate, and they can accept or reject the request or propose a new time for the meeting.

Create a Meeting in a Block of Time

① Click the Calendar icon on the Navigation Pane.

② Highlight a block of time on the meeting day for the meeting.

③ Click New Meeting on the Home tab.

(continued on next page)

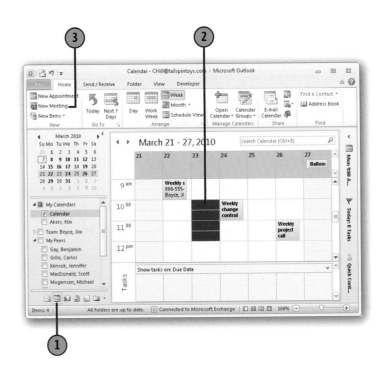

Tip ✓

You can use the Scheduling Assistant to help you find a time that is open for all invitees, and you can also identify available resources. To switch to the Scheduling Assistant view, click Scheduling Assistant in the Show group on the Meeting tab of the ribbon.

Create a Meeting in a Block of Time *(continued)*

④ Click To.

⑤ Select attendees and resources from the Address Book, or type the addresses manually.

⑥ Click Required if the invitee needs to attend.

⑦ Click Optional if the invitee isn't required to attend.

⑧ Click OK when you are done.

⑨ Type a description of the meeting in the Subject box.

⑩ Type the location of the meeting in the Location box.

⑪ Add notes, directions, or comments for the meeting as needed.

⑫ Click Send.

Try This!

When you type your meeting subject, keep it short but descriptive. "Team Meeting" may not be enough if people are members of multiple teams. Use something specific like "Development Team Meeting" for your description.

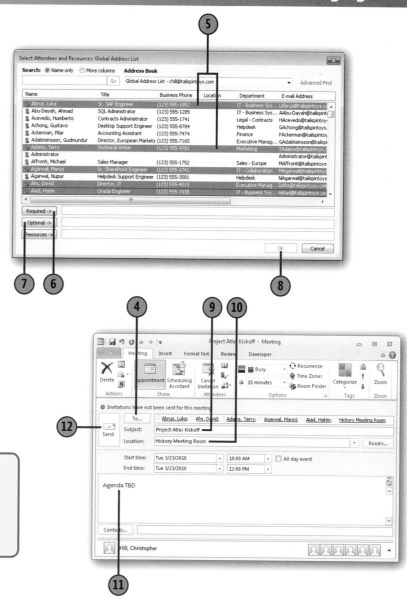

Change the Meeting Date and Time

Outlook uses the currently selected date and time by default when you create a new meeting request. You can change the date and time as you need to, rather than accept the default.

1. Create a new meeting.

2. Add attendees, a subject, and a location for the meeting.

3. Click the down arrow in the Start Time date field, and select the starting date.

4. Click the down arrow in the Start Time hour field, and select the starting time of the meeting.

5. Click the down arrow in the End Time hour field, and select the ending time of the meeting.

6. Click Send.

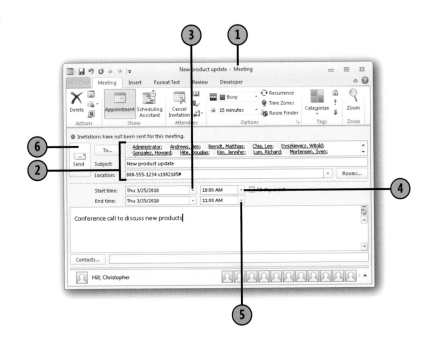

Caution

Make sure that your attendee list has correct e-mail addresses. If you attempt to send the meeting request to someone not in one of your address books, Outlook lets you know that the person can't be validated.

See Also

For information on the Address Book and adding new contacts, see Section 7, "Working with Contacts," starting on page 99.

Tip

Outlook provides the Scheduling Assistant to help you set up meetings with other people in your organization. The Scheduling Assistant lets you see other people's schedules if they have mailboxes in the same Exchange Server environment.

Updating Calendar Information

Outlook lets you edit a meeting, appointment, or event information saved in the Calendar folder. You might, for example, need to modify the time an appointment starts or ends, change where a meeting is held, or adjust the date of an event. When you change a meeting, you can send new meeting messages to attendees to announce the change.

Change an Appointment

① Click the Calendar icon on the Navigation Pane.

② Double-click the appointment you want to change. (If you open a recurring appointment, Outlook asks whether you want to change the occurrence or the series.)

③ Make changes to the appointment.

④ Click the Save & Close button.

Tip

Any date that has a meeting, appointment, or event appears in bold on the Date Navigator. Click that date to switch to the day, week, or month in which that activity occurs.

Try This!

Make an appointment recurring by clicking the Recurrence button and filling out the Appointment Recurrence information. For example, set the time for the appointment to occur from 8:00 A.M. to 10:00 A.M. every Thursday.

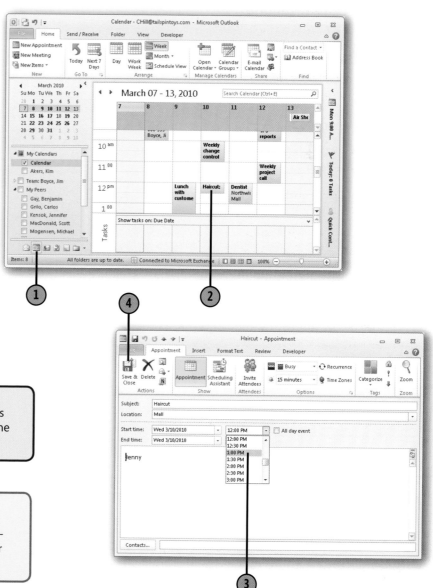

Update Event Information

① Click the Calendar icon on the Navigation Pane.

② Double-click the event you want to change.

③ Make changes to the event.

④ Click the Save & Close button.

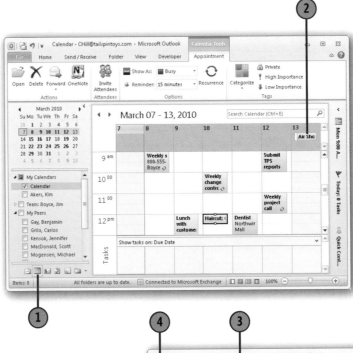

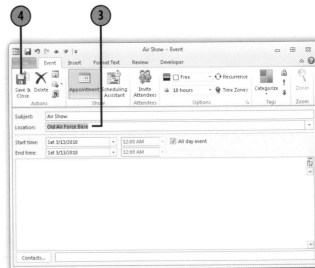

Reschedule a Meeting

① Open the meeting you want to change. If it is a recurring meeting, specify whether you want to change the occurrence or the series.

② Change the start day, if needed.

③ Click the Start Time hour drop-down list, and select the new start time.

④ Click the End Time hour drop-down list, and select the new end time.

⑤ Click Send Update.

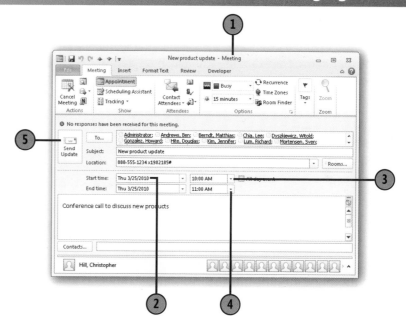

Tip

You can reschedule a meeting simply by dragging it to a new location on the Calendar. Regardless of the method you use to move the meeting, Outlook can automatically send an update to all attendees with notice of the new day and time.

Tip

Use the Tracking button on the Meeting tab to see which attendees have responded to your meeting request.

Inserting Items, Objects, and Files in a Calendar Item

Outlook enables you to insert objects, files, and Outlook items into your Calendar items. For example, you may have a meeting to which you want to take an important document or an agenda. You can insert the document into the meeting item so that you don't forget to take it with you and so that other attendees have a copy of it. You can add contacts from Outlook to a calendar item in much the same way.

Add an Outlook Item

① Open an appointment, meeting, or event.

② Click the Insert tab on the ribbon.

③ Click Outlook Item.

④ Select the Outlook folder in which the item is stored.

⑤ Select the Outlook item you want to insert from the Items list.

⑥ Click OK. The selected item now appears in the comment field.

⑦ Click the Meeting, Appointment, or Event tab, and then click Save & Close (for an appointment or event) or Send Update (for a meeting).

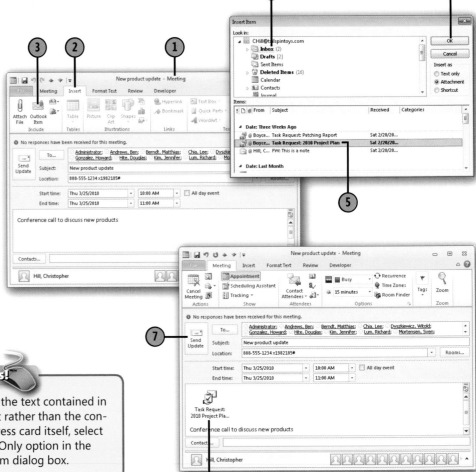

The selected item appears in the comment field.

Try This!

To insert the text contained in a contact rather than the contact address card itself, select the Text Only option in the Insert Item dialog box.

Add a File

① Double-click an appointment, meeting, or event.

② Click the Insert tab on the ribbon.

③ Click the Attach File button.

④ Select the file you want to insert.

⑤ Click Insert. The added file appears in the comment field.

⑥ Click the Meeting, Appointment, or Event tab, and then click Save & Close (or Send Update, for a meeting).

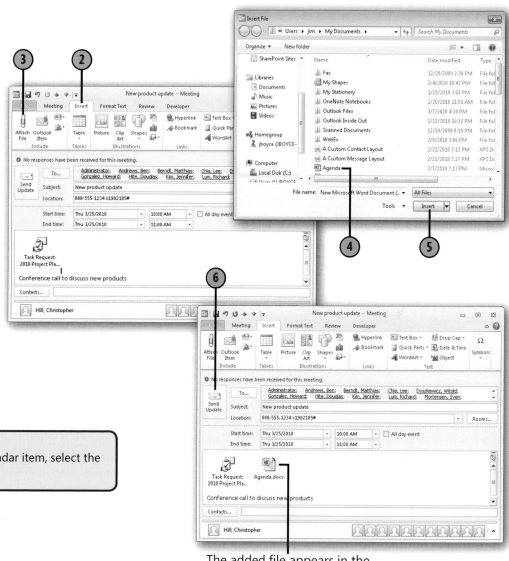

Tip

To delete a file, item, or object from a Calendar item, select the item and press Delete.

The added file appears in the comment field.

Add an Object from a File

1. Click the Calendar icon on the Navigation Pane.

2. Double-click an appointment, meeting, or event.

3. Click the Insert tab on the ribbon, and then click in the notes area of the item.

4. Click Object on the Text group of the ribbon's Insert tab.

5. Click the Create From File tab.

6. Click Browse.

(continued on next page)

Tip

Because you can add objects from a file, you can also embed a portion of a spreadsheet or other type of document in the appointment item for reference. For example, if you are discussing a project issue list in a meeting, you might embed the issue list from a Microsoft Excel spreadsheet in the meeting request so that the participants can review it before the meeting.

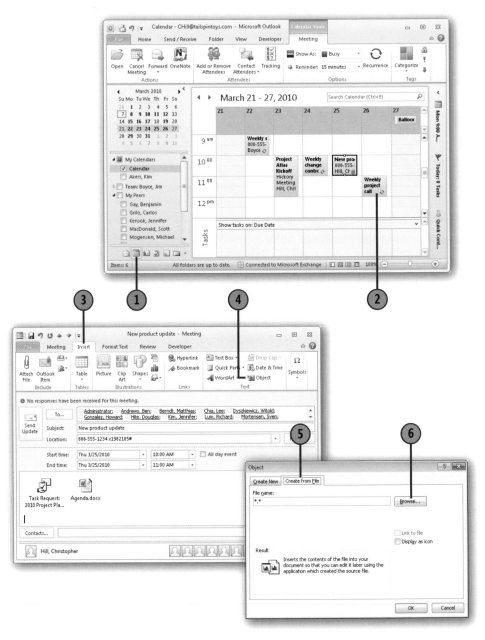

Add an Object from a File (continued)

⑦ In the dialog box, click the object you want to add.

⑧ Click Insert, and then click OK in the Object dialog box. The added object appears in the comment field.

⑨ Click the Appointment, Meeting, or Event tab, and then click Save & Close (or Send Update).

Tip

To create a new object, such as an Excel worksheet, select Create New in the Insert Object dialog box. When you click OK to insert the object, you then create the new object in that object's native application (such as Excel).

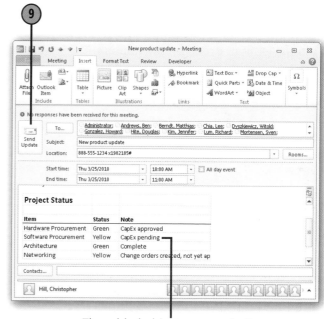

The added object appears in the comment field.

Working with Reminders

You can have Outlook display a reminder of upcoming appointments, events, or meetings. The reminder displays in a message box and can sound an alarm to alert you. You can use any sound included with Windows or use a sound that you've downloaded from the Internet and saved to your hard drive. Outlook adds a 15-minute reminder automatically when you create appointments or meetings, so you need to use the following process only if you want to add a reminder to an item that doesn't have one or when you want to change the reminder.

Add or Change a Reminder

1. Open the appointment, meeting, or event for which you want to set a reminder.

2. In the Options group on the ribbon's Appointment tab, choose a reminder time.

3. Click the Save & Close button. Outlook reminds you of the appointment at the scheduled time.

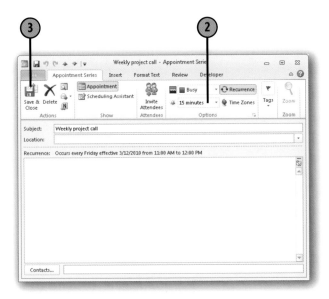

Tip

You can set up reminders for meetings and events by following the same sequence of steps shown here for appointments.

Tip

Reminders display even if the Calendar item is overdue. For example, if an event was set for Saturday and you didn't turn on your computer that day, the next time you start Windows, the reminder for that event appears. You can dismiss the reminder at that point.

Sharing Calendar Information

Outlook enables you to share Calendar information with others. You can forward a Calendar item by e-mail to other Outlook users, or you can forward an iCalendar item to any user of any Internet-connected mail program. You should use iCalendar when you schedule meetings with people who don't use Outlook.

Forward a Calendar Item

① Open an existing meeting item.

② Click the Meeting tab of the ribbon.

③ Click the Forward button.

④ Type the e-mail address of the recipient in the To box.

⑤ Click Send.

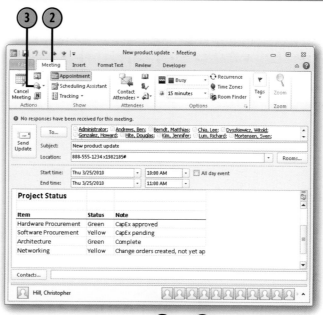

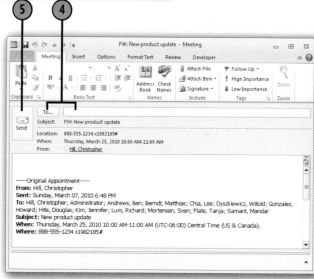

Forward an Item As iCalendar

① Open a meeting item by double-clicking it in the Calendar.

② Click the Meeting tab on the ribbon. This tab is named Meeting Series for a recurring meeting.

③ Click the arrow beside the Forward button.

④ Choose Forward As iCalendar. The item appears as an attachment.

⑤ Type the e-mail address of the recipient in the To box.

⑥ Click Send.

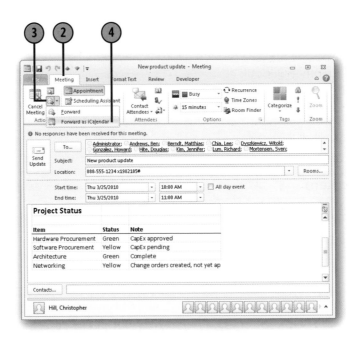

Tip

If you forward a calendar item that has an attachment, that attachment is forwarded along with the calendar item.

Tip

iCalendar is for communicating with people who don't use Outlook. If you want to forward a Calendar item to someone who uses Outlook, use the Forward command on the Actions menu or click Forward in the Actions group on the meeting form's ribbon.

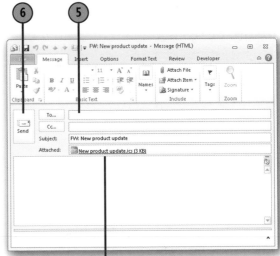

The item appears as an attachment.

Printing Calendars

You can print your Outlook appointment calendar, such as your daily or weekly appointments, meetings, and events. Or you can print an individual calendar item, such as a meeting item.

Print your Appointment Calendar

(1) Click the Calendar icon on the Navigation Pane, and then click File.

(2) Choose Print.

(3) Choose a calendar style in the Print Style area.

(4) Click Print.

Tip

You can print your calendars in Daily, Weekly, Monthly, Tri-fold, Calendar Detail, and Memo Style. Print your calendar in each one of these styles and pick your favorite one.

Try This!

Print your appointment calendar at the beginning of each week so that you can keep track of all your upcoming events, appointments, and meetings. As schedules change, such as a meeting being delayed or canceled, make these changes on the hard copy as well as in Outlook. If too many changes happen, of course, you need to print a fresh calendar.

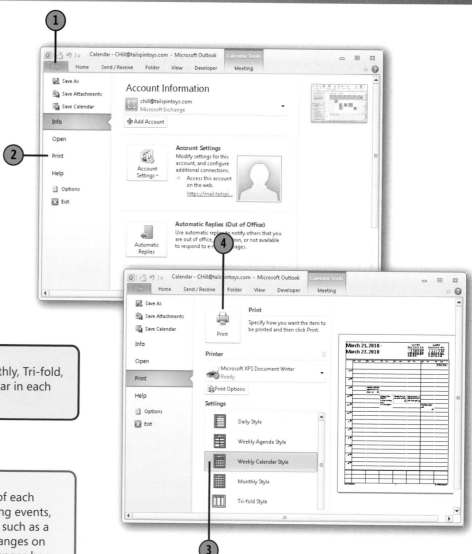

Print a Calendar Item

① Click the Calendar icon on the Navigation Pane.

② Double-click the Calendar item you want to print.

③ Click File.

④ Click Print.

⑤ Set print options.

⑥ Click Print.

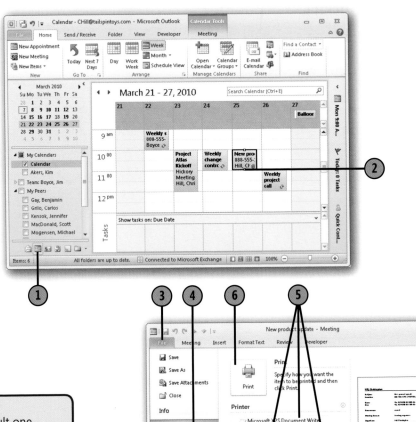

Tip

If you want to print to a printer other than the default one, click the Printer drop-down list and select the printer.

Try This!

Print a Calendar item that has an attachment inserted in it. Click Print Options, and when the Print dialog box appears, select Print Attached Files to print the attachment.

Working with Tasks

Most of us at some time or another have written a to-do list—a list of tasks we need to perform. Maybe you put together a list of the improvements or repairs you want to make to your house. Maybe it's something simpler like a list of errands to run. Whatever the case, having a list of the tasks you need to complete can be valuable for keeping you on track.

Microsoft Outlook 2010 includes a feature to help you keep your list in mind. The Tasks folder stores your to-do list. You can create tasks for yourself, assign them a due date, and easily mark them as completed. You can create one-time tasks or recurring tasks. Outlook also lets you assign tasks to others and receive status updates on the tasks from the people to whom you assign them. This section explains how to use the Tasks folder to create and manage one-time and recurring tasks, as well as assign tasks to others.

Viewing Your Tasks

Outlook includes a Tasks folder that you can use to store your tasks and tasks that you assign to others. The Tasks folder offers a handful of ways to view and work with your tasks, including the Daily Task List that appears at the bottom of the Calendar, and the Tasks List in the To-Do Bar. The default view for the Tasks folder is the Simple List view, which shows whether the task is complete, the name (subject) of the task, and the due date.

Open the Task Item Window

① Click the Tasks icon on the Navigation Pane to open the Tasks folder.

② Double-click a task to open the task's form. If you don't have a task created yet, just double-click in the Tasks folder to start a new task.

③ Click Details in the Show group of the ribbon's Task tab to display additional task information.

④ Click the Save & Close button to close the form.

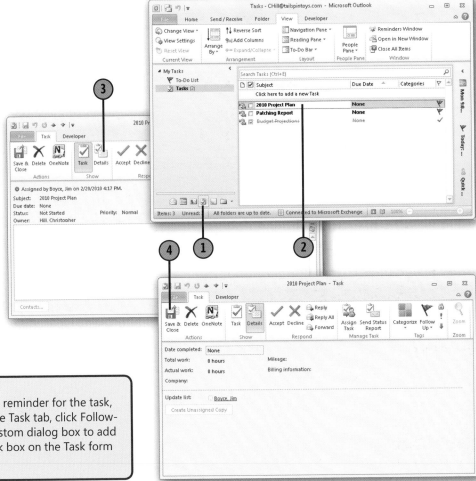

> **Tip**
>
> Outlook provides several different views for the Tasks folder, and you can easily create your own views to suit your needs.

> **Tip**
>
> When you create a task, Outlook doesn't set up a reminder for the task, but you can add one later. Open the task, click the Task tab, click Follow-Up, Add Reminder, and then use the resulting Custom dialog box to add a reminder. You can also click the Reminder check box on the Task form and set a reminder directly on the form.

Use the Task List

(1) In Outlook, click the Tasks icon on the Navigation Pane to open the Tasks folder.

(2) When the Tasks folder opens, click the Subject column to sort the list by Subject.

(3) Click Due Date to restore the default sort method.

(4) Click the flag beside the task's subject to mark the task as complete.

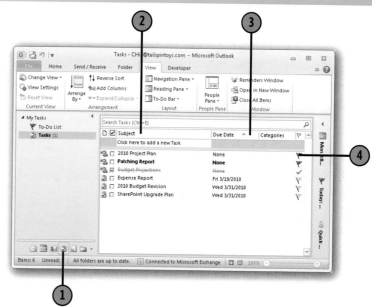

Tip

You can add and remove columns from the Task List to show the task data most important to you. Right-click the column header, and select Field Chooser. In the Field Chooser dialog box, click a column and drag it to the column header. To remove a column, drag it from the column header to the Field Chooser dialog box. Note that you must widen some views or turn off the Reading Pane to accomplish this with some views (such as the To-Do Bar).

Tip

If you don't see the To-Do Bar, click To-Do Bar on the View tab of the ribbon and choose Normal.

Tip

If you're using a view that includes the Complete check box, just click the check box to mark a task as complete.

Use the Task List in the Calendar

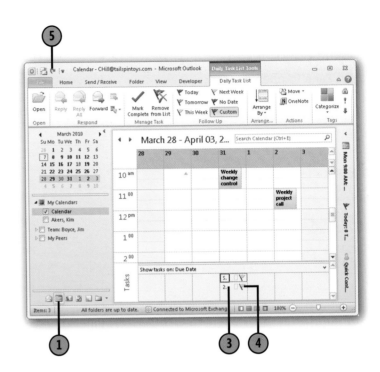

1. Click the Calendar icon on the Navigation Pane to open the Calendar folder.

2. Click the Day or Week button on the Home tab.

3. View the tasks in the Task List.

4. Click the flag beside a task to mark it as complete.

5. Choose Undo Flag from the Quick Access Toolbar (or press Ctrl+Z) to restore the task to the list.

Tip

If you can't see the To-Do Bar, click the View tab, click To-Do Bar, and then choose Normal.

See Also

The Outlook Today view is built using HTML, the same language used to design Web pages. If you have some knowledge of HTML, you can create a custom Outlook Today view. See *Microsoft® Outlook® 2010 Inside Out,* by Jim Boyce (Microsoft Press, 2010), to learn more about customizing the Outlook Today view.

Tip

The Outlook Today view includes a simplified task list that shows the subject and completion status. You can click on a task's subject to open the task to view its details or modify it. Click the check box beside a task to mark it as complete.

Adding a Task

Tasks can be added to your Tasks folder in one of two ways: You can create the task yourself or accept a task that someone else assigns to you. If you create the task yourself, you can create it by using the New Items button on the Home tab for any folder, or you can create it through the Tasks folder.

Set the Task Name and Due Date

1. Click the Tasks icon on the Navigation Pane to open the Tasks folder.

2. Click New Task to start a new task.

3. Type a subject for the task.

4. Click the arrow beside the Due Date field and select a date from the date navigator.

5. Click Save & Close.

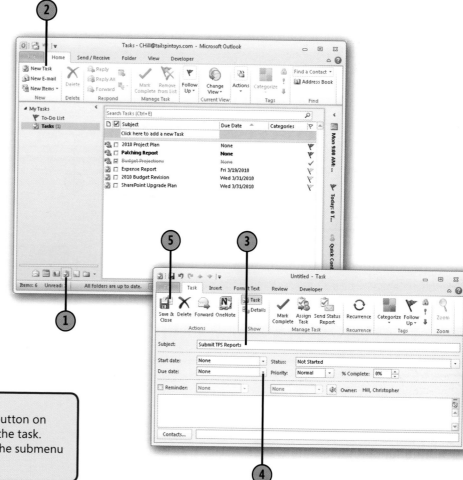

Tip

With any folder open, you can use the New Items button on the Home tab to open a new task form and create the task. Click the New Items button and choose Task from the submenu to open the new task form.

Set or Change Task Properties

① Click the Tasks icon on the Navigation Pane to open the Tasks folder.

② Double-click the task whose properties you want to change to open the task form.

(continued on next page)

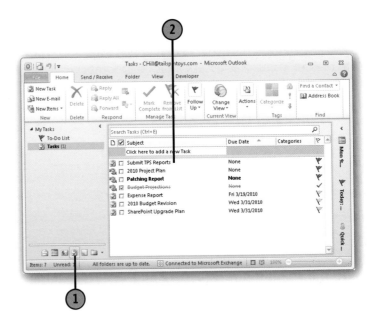

Tip

Outlook makes a connection between the Status and % Complete properties. If you specify some percentage less than 100% in the % Complete field, Outlook changes the Status field to In Progress. Setting % Complete to 0 changes Status to Not Started. Setting % Complete to 100% causes Outlook to set Status to Completed. Likewise, setting Status to Completed sets % Complete to 100%.

Try This!

If you delegate an Outlook folder to other users, allowing them to open your folder and view the items in it, they can see all items not marked private. Use the Private button in the Tags group of the ribbon's Task tab to prevent your delegates from seeing the task in your task list.

Set or Change Task Properties *(continued)*

③ Click the Task tab, if you need to.

④ Modify the start and end dates as you like.

⑤ Click the Status drop-down list and choose a status, such as Started, In Progress, or Completed.

⑥ Select a priority from the Priority drop-down list.

⑦ Specify the percent complete in the % Complete field.

⑧ Click the Details button.

⑨ Set additional properties for the task.

⑩ Click Save & Close to close the form.

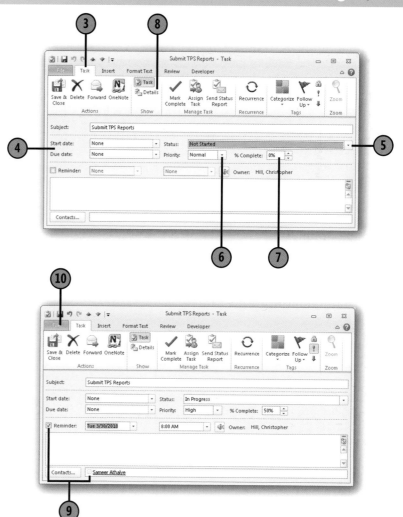

> **Tip** ✓
>
> When you set a reminder for a task, Outlook assigns the default sound for the reminder, and Outlook plays that sound and displays the reminder in the Reminders dialog box when the specified time arrives. You can click the Speaker button next to the Reminder date and time fields to select a different sound file for Outlook to play when it displays the reminder.

> **See Also**
>
> For more information on working with reminders, see "Working with Reminders" on page 144.

Working with Recurring Tasks

Some tasks are recurring tasks—they repeat on a regular basis. For example, maybe you have to prepare a set of reports every Friday that summarizes the week's sales or other information. Or perhaps you need to back up your files every week. Although a recurring task shows up only once in the task list, it appears in the Tasks lists in the Calendar and on the To-Do Bar when the assigned due date falls in the list's range. If you set a reminder for the task, you receive the reminder for each recurrence of the task.

Create a Recurring Task

1. Click the Tasks icon on the Navigation Pane to open the Tasks folder.

2. Click New Task on the Home tab to open a form for the new task (or edit an existing task).

(continued on next page)

Tip

If you set a recurring task with no end date, you can still revise the task's properties to make it end after a specified number of occurrences or specified date. Just open the task's properties, click Recurrence to open the Task Recurrence dialog box, choose the end option that you want, and click OK. Then click Save & Close to save the changes.

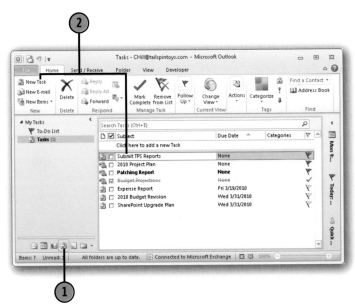

Create a Recurring Task *(continued)*

(3) Set the Subject, Start Date, and other information for the task.

(4) Click Recurrence in the Options group of the ribbon's Task tab to open the Task Recurrence dialog box.

(5) Select the type of recurrence.

(6) Specify how often the task should recur, or specify that Outlook should create the new task after the current one is complete.

(7) Set the start and end of the recurrence period.

(8) Click OK.

(9) Click Save & Close to close the task's form.

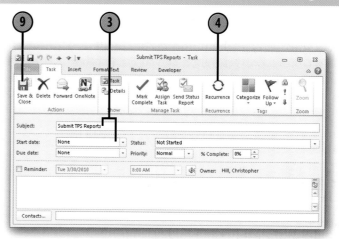

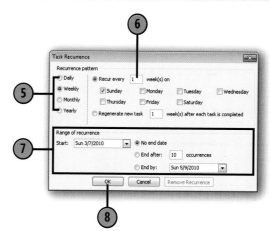

Try This!

You can make a recurring task nonrecurring by opening a task's form, clicking Recurrence on the toolbar to open the Task Recurrence dialog box, and then clicking Remove Recurrence.

Tip

Select the Recur Every option in the Task Recurrence dialog box when you want the task to recur even if the previous occurrence hasn't been completed. Select the Regenerate New Task option if you want the task to recur only after the last occurrence is complete.

Modifying and Updating a Task

You can modify a task at any time to change any property, including subject, due date, recurrence, and so on. Another change you might want to make to tasks is to mark them as complete. This action allows you to see at a glance the tasks that are complete and those that are not. You can also change the view of the Tasks folder to show only tasks that are complete, only tasks that are overdue, only those that are incomplete, and so on. In addition to marking tasks complete, you probably want to delete completed tasks and send status updates for tasks that are assigned to you.

Mark a Task As Complete

① Click the Tasks icon on the Navigation Pane to open the Tasks folder.

② Click the View tab.

③ Click Change View.

④ Choose Simple List.

⑤ Click the check box in the Complete column to mark a task as complete.

⑥ Note that Outlook displays completed tasks using strikethrough.

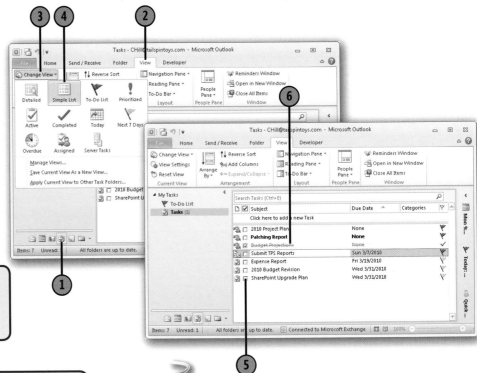

Tip

You can click the check box next to a task on the Tasks List (Day, Week, or Work Week views in the Calendar) to mark a task as complete.

Tip

You can mark tasks complete in any task view; these steps introduce you to the Simple List view as a means for viewing all tasks as a list, as well as marking tasks complete. If your current view doesn't include a Complete column, you can right-click a task and choose Mark Complete.

Try This!

You can mark a task complete by setting its percent complete value to 100%. Open the task and use the arrow button beside the % Complete option to set the value to 100%. Outlook marks the task as complete.

Delete a Completed Task

1 Select the task in any folder where the task is visible.

2 Click the Delete button on the Standard toolbar to delete the task.

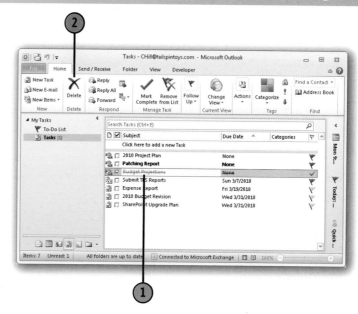

Tip

When you delete a task, Outlook places the task in the Deleted Items folder. If you delete the wrong task or decide you don't want to delete it after all, you can restore it to the Tasks folder. Using the Folder List in the Navigation Pane, open the Deleted Items folder and drag the task to the Tasks icon. You can also right-click a task in the Deleted Items folder, choose Move, Other Folder, select the Tasks folder, and click OK to move it back.

Tip

You can delete any task, whether or not the task is marked as complete. Use the same method to delete an incomplete task that you use to delete a complete task.

Send a Status Report for an Assigned Task

1. Click the Tasks icon on the Navigation Pane to open the Tasks folder.

2. Double-click the task to open its form.

3. Make changes to the task's properties as needed.

4. Click the Save button to save the changes.

5. Click Send Status Report in the Manage Task group of the ribbon's Task tab.

(continued on next page)

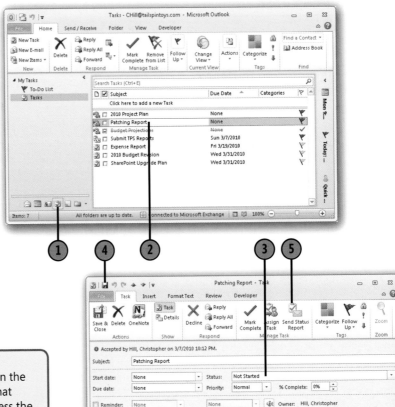

Try This!

You can send a copy of a status report to a person not on the update list without letting the people on the list know that you've copied that person. Just use the Bcc field to address the message to the other person. If Outlook isn't currently showing the Bcc field, choose Show Bcc from the Show Fields group under the Options tab.

See Also

For more information on assigning tasks to others, see "Assigning a Task to Someone Else" on page 166.

Send a Status Report for an Assigned Task *(continued)*

(6) Outlook adds the update address list (person who assigned the task to you); click To or Cc to add addresses for people not included in the update list.

(7) Click in the body of the message and add notes or comments as you like.

(8) Click Send to send the message.

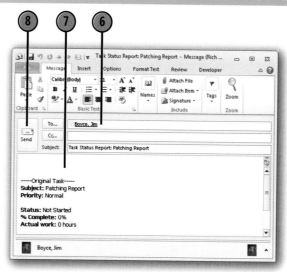

See Also

For more information on adding and editing text in a message form, see "Changing Message Text" on page 55.

Tip

Outlook fills in the status information in the body of the update message for you. You can edit this text if you need to. Just highlight the text you want to change, and type the replacement text.

See Also

For more information on addressing e-mail messages and working with the address book, see "Writing an E-Mail Message" on page 48.

Inserting Items into a Task

When you create a task—whether you create the task for yourself or assign it to someone else—you might want to add items to the task. For example, assume you're going to assign a task to someone else, and that person needs a copy of a Word document to perform the task. You can attach the document to the task. Or perhaps you need to include some contacts with a task. Whatever the case, it's easy to insert Outlook items, objects, and files in a task.

Add an Outlook Item

1 Click the Tasks icon on the Navigation Pane to open the Tasks folder.

2 Double-click a task to open its form.

3 Click the Insert tab on the ribbon.

4 Click in the notes area of the Task.

5 In the Include group, click Outlook Item.

(continued on next page)

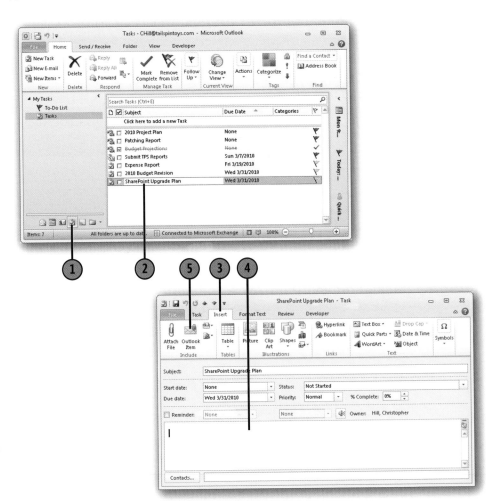

Add an Outlook Item (continued)

6 Select the Outlook folder that contains the object you want to insert.

7 Select the item to insert.

8 Select an option to specify how to insert the object.

9 Click OK.

10 Click the Task tab, and then click Save & Close.

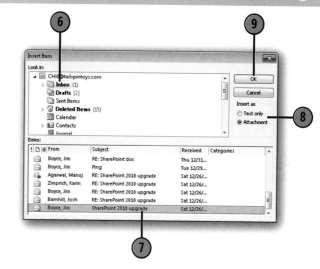

An item inserted as an attachment

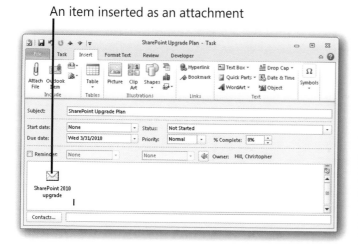

An item inserted as text only

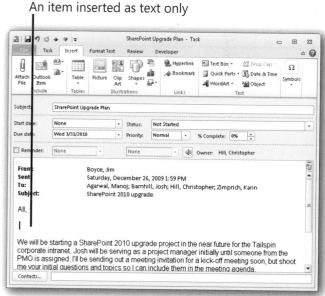

Add a File

① Click the Tasks icon to open the Tasks folder.

② Double-click a task to open its form.

③ Click the Insert tab on the ribbon.

④ Click the Attach File button in the Include group.

(continued on next page)

See Also

For more information about attaching files to e-mail messages rather than adding them to tasks, see "E-Mailing a File" on page 64.

Tip

When you insert a file as a hyperlink, Outlook inserts the path to the document. If you insert a file from your local computer, the path uses the local drive letter. This method works fine for creating hyperlinks to documents you use, but it doesn't work when you assign tasks to other people because clicking the link on their end causes Outlook to try to open the file from their computers. However, you can link files on network servers in tasks that you assign, as long as you view the server through a universal naming convention (UNC) path rather than a mapped drive. A UNC path takes the form \\server\folder, where *server* is the name of the server and *folder* the name of the shared folder on the server on which the document is located. Likewise, you can link to a file on a SharePoint site by copying the URL for the SharePoint item into the task.

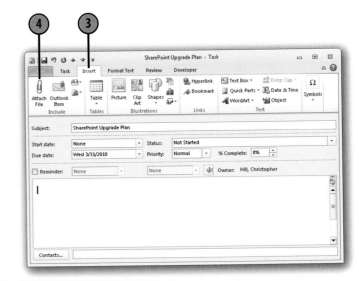

Add a File   *(continued)*

⑤ Select the file you want to insert.

⑥ Click Insert to insert the file.

⑦ The file appears as an icon in the task.

⑧ Add other information to the task as you need to.

⑨ Click Task, and then click Save & Close.

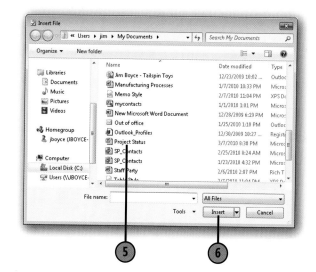

Tip

You can insert a file as a hyperlink rather than as an attachment, which allows the task to be opened from its source rather than included in the task. The main benefit of this method is that you don't duplicate the document but instead create a shortcut to it. The limitation is that everyone who receives the message must have access to wherever the file is stored. To insert a hyperlink in a task, open the task and click Attach File on the Insert tab. Select the file, click the arrow beside the Insert button, and then choose Insert As Hyperlink.

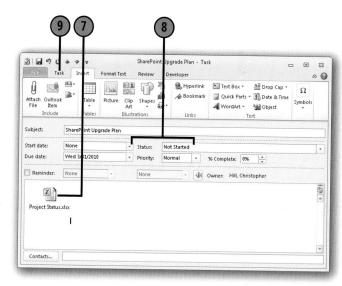

Assigning a Task to Someone Else

If you manage others and use Outlook in your organization for e-mail and collaboration, you probably want to assign tasks to others. Outlook sends the task assignment as an e-mail message, and the assignee has the option of accepting or rejecting the task. When you assign a task, you define a status update distribution list. The people on that list receive status reports when the assignee makes changes to the task.

Assign a Task

① Click New Items on the Home tab.

② Choose Task Request.

(continued on next page)

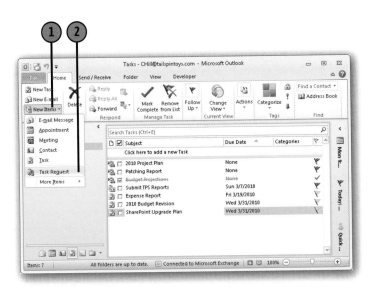

Try This!

If you want to pass the buck and reassign a task that was assigned to you to someone else, accept the task, open the task, click Assign Task in the Manage Task group of the ribbon's Task tab, and assign it by typing someone's name or selecting a name from your address list.

See Also

For information on how to include a document with a task you assign to someone else, see "Inserting Items into a Task" on page 162.

Tip

When you assign a task to another person, a copy of the task request message goes into your Sent Items folder. If you open the message, its form shows a status message indicating that Outlook is waiting for a response from the assignee. This message changes after the assignee either accepts or rejects the task.

Assign a Task   *(continued)*

③ Use the fields on the Task tab to define the task.

④ Select Keep An Updated Copy Of This Task On My Task List to have Outlook keep track of the assigned task with a copy on your own task list that updates as the assignee works on the task.

⑤ Select Send Me A Status Report When This Task Is Complete to have Outlook send you a status report when the assignee completes the task.

⑥ Type the assignee's name, or click To and select the person to whom you want to assign the task from your Contacts list.

⑦ Click the Details button.

⑧ Add other information for the task.

⑨ Click Task to return to the task form.

⑩ Click Send.

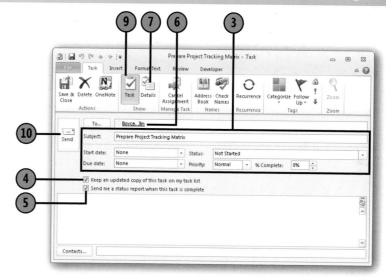

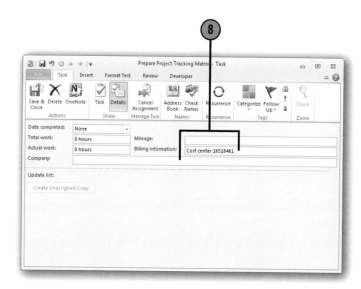

Accept or Reject an Assigned Task

1. Click the Mail icon on the Navigation Pane and open the Inbox.

2. Click the Task Request message to select it. If the Preview Pane is not open, double-click the message to open it.

3. Click Accept to accept the task or Decline to decline the task.

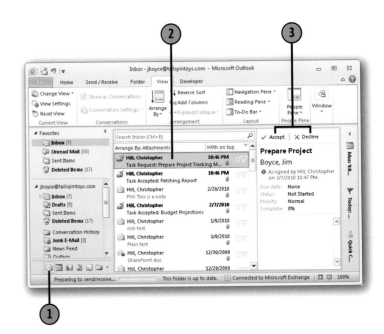

Sharing Task Information

Sometimes you might need to share a task with someone else. For example, you might need to include information about a task in a written report. Or perhaps you need to print a list of tasks to include in an information packet for a staff meeting. Outlook gives you several ways to share tasks, including printing them and sending them through e-mail messages.

Print a Task List

1 Open the Tasks folder tab and then click the File tab.

2 Click Print.

3 In the Print dialog box, choose the printer to which you want to print the list.

4 Select Table Style from the Print Style menu.

5 Click Print to print the list.

Try This!

Sometimes you might not want to include all of your tasks in the printed list. Open the Tasks folder, hold down the Ctrl key, and click on the tasks you want included in the list. Choose Print from the File tab, select the printer, click Print Options, and then select Only Selected Rows. Click OK, then Print to print the selected tasks.

See Also

For more information on printing your schedule, see "Printing Calendars" on page 147.

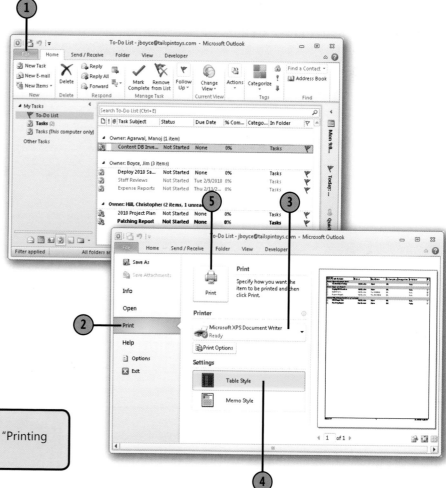

Print a Task Item

1. Open the Tasks folder, and open the task you want to print.

2. Click the File tab.

3. Click Print.

4. Click Print Options.

5. Choose the number of copies you need to print.

6. Select the Print Attached Files option if you want to also print any attached files along with the task.

7. Click Print to print the task.

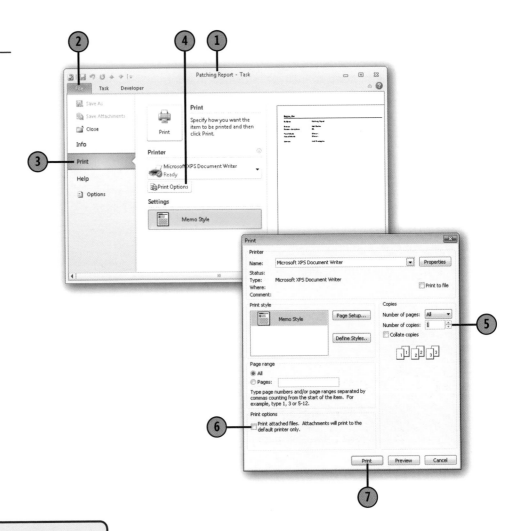

Tip

If you don't need to set any printing options but just want to quickly print a task, right-click the task in the task list and choose Quick Print. Outlook sends the task to the printer without prompting for any other information.

See Also

For more information about attaching files to a task, see "Add a File" on page 164.

Forward a Task

(1) Open the Tasks folder, and right-click a task.

(2) Choose Forward to open a message with the task as an attachment.

(3) Select the recipient for the message.

(4) Add notes or other comments in the body of the message.

(5) Click Send to send the message.

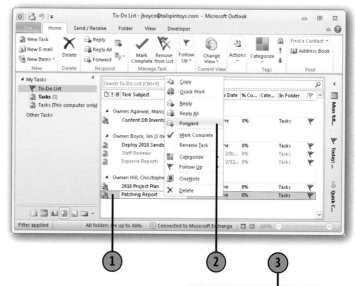

See Also

For more information on composing e-mail messages, see "Writing an E-Mail Message" on page 48.

Tip

You can forward a task from the task window as well as from the Tasks folder. With the task open, choose Forward from the Respond group of the Task tab.

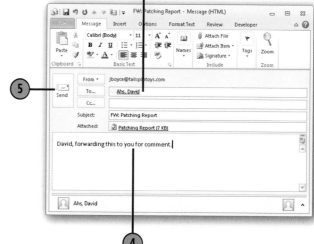

Using Alerts and Mobile Features

Microsoft Outlook 2010 offers some great mobility features to help you integrate Outlook with your mobile devices. In particular, you can configure Outlook to send alerts to your cell phone, pocket PC, or other mobile devices when you receive important e-mail or voice messages. Outlook can also send you reminders about appointments and meetings and a daily summary of your day's schedule. These features can help you arrive at your meetings on time and stay abreast of important e-mail when you're out of the office.

Configuring Mobile Alert Settings for Exchange Server Accounts

Before you can receive alerts on your mobile device, you must configure your Exchange Server account settings to specify your mobile device number.

① Click File.

② Click Account Settings, and then click Manage Mobile Notifications.

③ Enter your user name and password.

④ Click Sign In.

⑤ Click Phone.

⑥ Click Text Messaging.

⑦ Click Turn On Notifications.

(continued on next page)

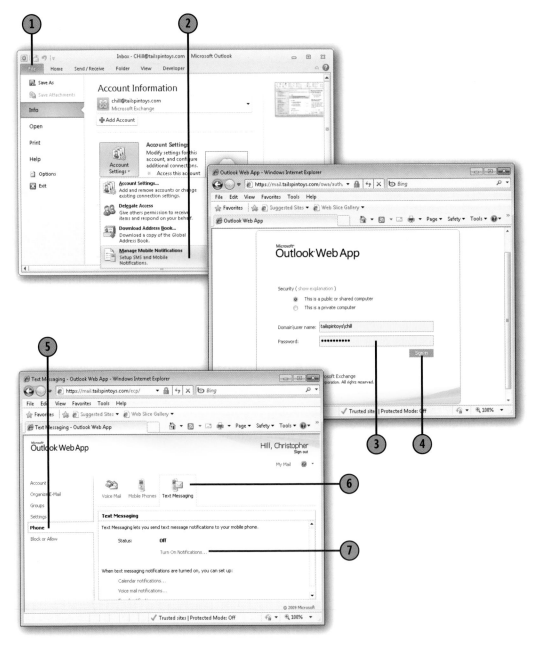

Tip

If the Manage Mobile Notifications option is missing from the Account Settings menu in Outlook, open Internet Explorer and browse to *https://YourMailServer/ecp*, where YourMailServer is the address of your Exchange Server. And then log in as indicated in step 3.

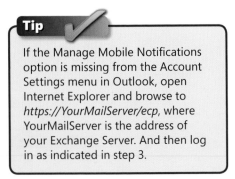

Configuring Mobile Alert Settings for Exchange Server Accounts *(continued)*

(8) Select your locale.

(9) Select your mobile provider.

(10) Click Next.

(11) Enter your mobile device number.

(12) Click Next.

(13) Exchange Server sends a text message, which includes a code, to your mobile device; enter that code in the Passcode field.

(14) Click Finish.

Tip ✓

The e-mail and calendar alert features described in this chapter require a Microsoft Exchange Server 2010 mailbox. The voice mail alerts also require that the mailbox user be enabled for unified messaging.

Tip ✓

Exchange Server sends a text message to your mobile device to let you know when you have successfully completed the alert setup process.

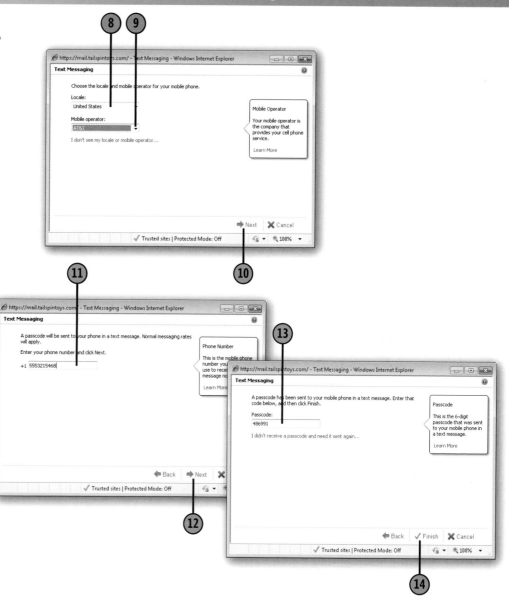

Setting Up Calendar Alerts

Using Calendar alerts, you can have Exchange Server send alerts to your mobile device when new items are added to your calendar or existing items are updated. This feature is particularly helpful when you're out of the office and an assistant is scheduling or accepting meetings for you. You can also have Exchange Server send reminders for meetings to your mobile device. In addition, you can configure your alert settings to have Exchange Server send a summary of your daily calendar agenda to your mobile device, giving you an easy reference to what's on your schedule for that day. These three features combined can keep you plugged into your schedule all day, even when you're away from your computer.

1. Click File.

2. Click Account Settings, and then click Manage Mobile Notifications.

3. Enter your user name and password.

4. Click Sign In.

(continued on next page)

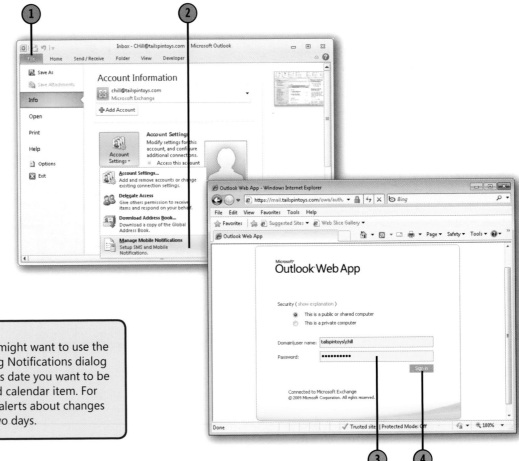

Tip

If your schedule changes frequently, you might want to use the drop-down control on the Text Messaging Notifications dialog box to specify how many days ahead of its date you want to be notified or reminded of a new or changed calendar item. For example, choose 2 if you want to receive alerts about changes that affect your calendar over the next two days.

Setting Up Calendar Alerts *(continued)*

⑤ Click Phone.

⑥ Click Text Messaging.

⑦ Click Set Up Calendar Notifications.

⑧ Choose Notifications When My Calendar Is Updated In The Next n Days to receive a notification whenever your calendar is updated with new or changed items in the specified time period.

⑨ Specify the number of days ahead in your schedule for which you want to be notified.

⑩ Choose Send Only During Working Hours if you want to receive notifications only during working hours.

⑪ Choose Notifications For Meeting Reminders if you want to receive meeting reminders on your mobile device.

⑫ Choose Send Only During Working Hours if you want to receive notifications only during working hours.

⑬ Choose Daily Calendar Agendas to receive a summary of your daily schedule.

⑭ Choose the time at which you want to receive the agenda summary.

⑮ Click Save.

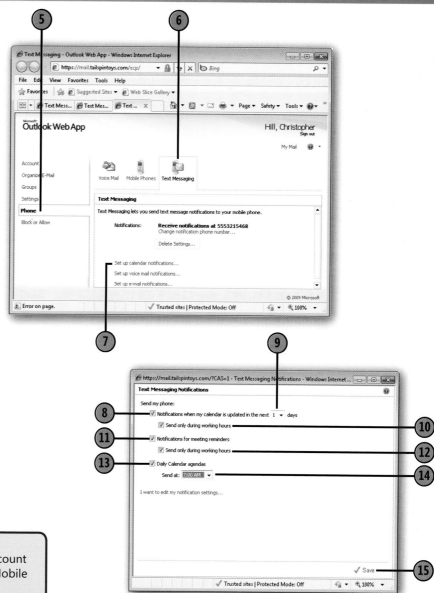

Tip

Keep in mind that you don't need an Exchange Server account to be able to send mobile alerts. If you add an Outlook Mobile Service account, Outlook can send the alerts.

Setting Up Mobile Alerts for Important Messages

If you have a mobile device that synchronizes your mailbox to your mobile device, you likely receive e-mail on the device all day long. If not, you might want to configure Exchange Server to send an alert to your mobile device when you receive certain types of messages. For example, you might want it to send you an alert when you receive an e-mail from your manager, receive an e-mail from an incident management system, or receive e-mail with specific words in the subject, related to a particular project.

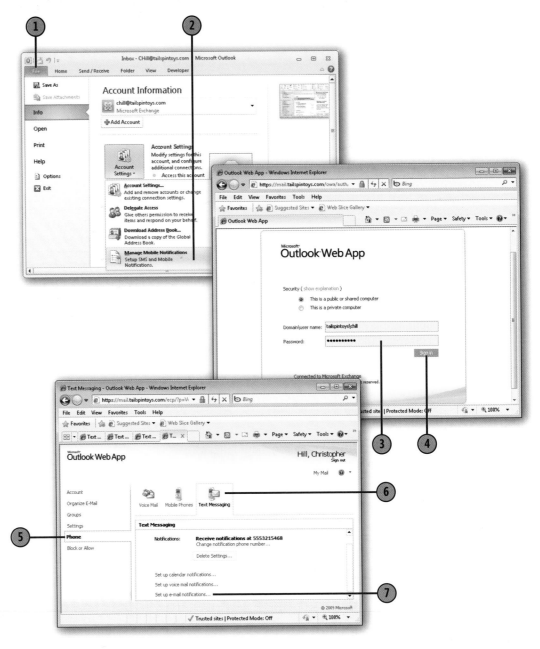

1. Click File.

2. Click Account Settings, and then click Manage Mobile Notifications.

3. Enter your user name and password.

4. Click Sign In.

5. Click Phone.

6. Click Text Messaging.

7. Click Set Up E-Mail Notifications

(continued on next page)

Setting Up Mobile Alerts for Important Messages *(continued)*

⑧ Choose the condition for the alert rule. This example assumes you're creating a rule to alert you when you receive an e-mail from a specific person.

⑨ Click to open the Address Book (if it does not open automatically).

⑩ In the Address Book, choose the person for whose e-mails you want to be alerted.

⑪ Click From.

⑫ Click OK.

⑬ Choose Send A Text Message To.

⑭ Click to choose the mobile device number to which you want alerts sent.

⑮ Click Save.

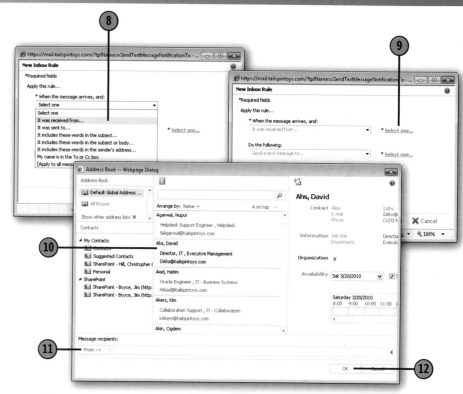

Tip ✓

Even if your mobile device synchronizes with your Exchange mailbox and you receive all e-mail on your mobile device, you might still want to set up alerts. If you receive a lot of e-mail during the day, you probably have configured your mobile device not to alert you when you receive an e-mail. You can create the alert for the types of messages for which you do want to receive notification, and then configure your mobile device to notify with a sound or vibration when you receive a text message. When you get the alert from Exchange Server, you can scroll through the e-mail you've already received to find the one for which you received the alert.

Tip ✓

You can click More Options to expand the dialog box to show options that let you add exceptions to the rule. For example, you might add an exception if the message is marked as low priority so that you don't receive alerts for those messages. Or, you might add an exception for messages for which your name is in the Cc field so that you receive alerts only for messages that were sent directly to you.

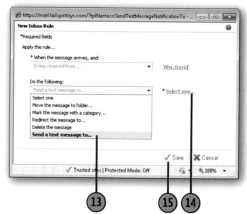

Setting Up a Text Messaging Service

If you have an SMS service account, you can configure that account in Outlook so that you can send text messages from Outlook. This practice is handy when you're in front of your computer most of the day but still need to send text messages to colleagues or friends. You also might find it easier to compose the text message in Outlook, thanks to your computer's full keyboard. The first step in sending text messages from Outlook is to set up the account.

Add an Outlook Mobile Service Account

1. Click File.

2. Click Account Settings, and then click Account Settings.

3. Click New.

(continued on next page)

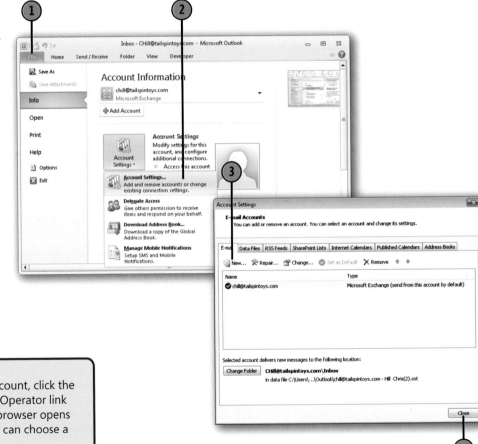

Tip

If you don't already have an Outlook Mobile Account, click the Find A Text Messaging Service For Your Mobile Operator link on the Account Settings dialog box. Your Web browser opens on a page at the Microsoft Web site, where you can choose a provider.

Add an Outlook Mobile Service
Account *(continued)*

④ Click Text Messaging (SMS).

⑤ Click Next.

⑥ Enter the service provider's URL.

⑦ Enter your user ID for the service.

⑧ Enter the password for the ID.

⑨ Click OK.

⑩ Click Finish.

⑪ Click Close in the Account Settings
dialog box.

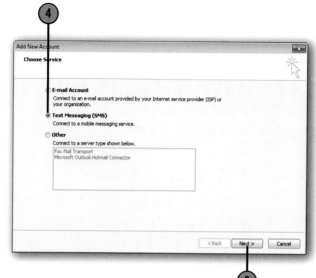

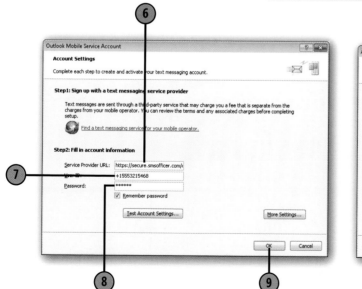

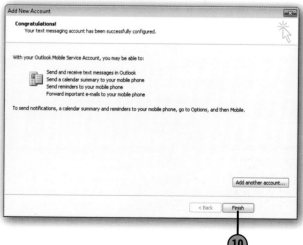

Sending Text Messages from Outlook

After you have configured an SMS account in Outlook, you can use it to send text messages from Outlook. The process is as simple as sending an e-mail, although a bit different.

(1) In Outlook, click the Mail icon.

(2) Click New Items and choose Text Message (SMS).

(3) Choose the recipient from the Address Book.

(4) Type the text for the message.

(5) Preview the message.

(6) Click Send to send the message.

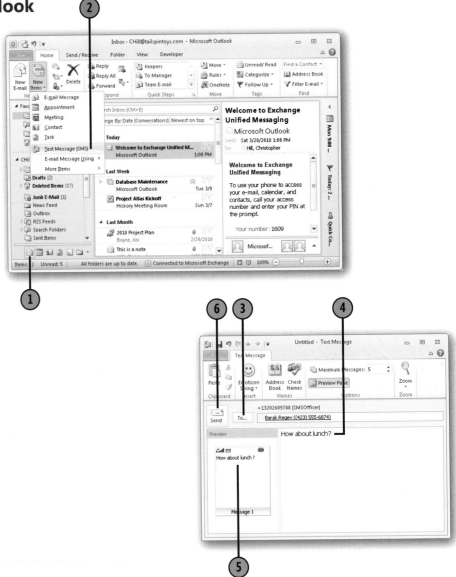

Sending Mobile Alerts from Outlook

You don't need an Exchange Server account to send mobile alerts, such as calendar reminders, to forward e-mail messages to your mobile device. If you have added an Outlook Mobile Service account to your profile, you can configure Outlook to send alerts and forward messages. However, Outlook must be running and have an Internet connection available for you to use these features.

Set Up a Mobile Calendar Summary

After you have set up an Outlook Mobile Service account, you can forward calendar alerts from Outlook.

1. Click File.

2. Click Options.

3. Click Mobile.

4. Click Calendar Summary Settings.

5. Select Send A Calendar Summary To A Mobile Device.

6. Change the mobile device number, if needed.

7. Specify how much of the calendar to include in the summary.

8. Specify when the summary should be sent.

9. Set other options as needed.

10. Click OK.

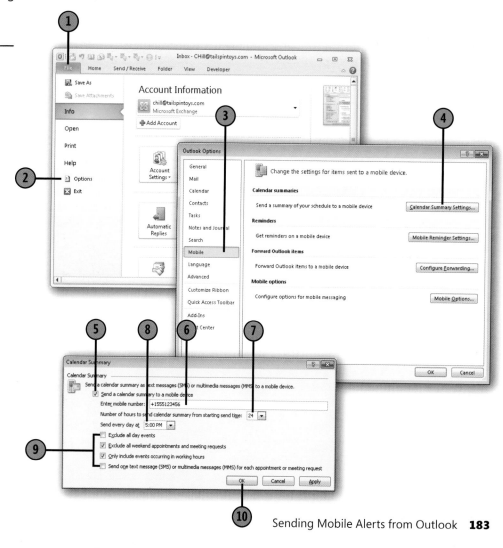

Set Up Mobile Reminders

1 On the Mobile page of the Outlook Options dialog box, click Mobile Reminder Settings.

2 Click Send Reminders.

3 Verify or change your mobile number.

4 Set additional options as needed.

5 Click OK.

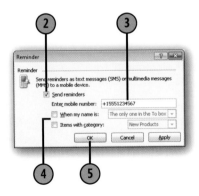

Configure Message Forwarding

1 On the Mobile page of the Outlook Options dialog box, click Configure Forwarding.

2 Select Forward Outlook Items That Meet All Of The Selected Conditions.

3 Verify or change your mobile number.

4 Specify conditions to identify the messages that you want forwarded to you.

5 Click OK.

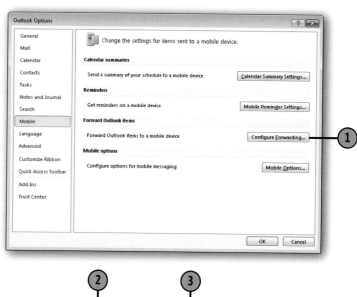

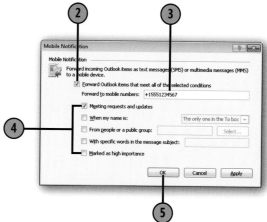

Using Outlook with SharePoint and OCS

11

Microsoft SharePoint has rapidly become a popular solution for collaboration, allowing users to share documents, calendars, contacts, and other information among teams or across entire organizations. When you add SharePoint's process automation and business intelligence features, SharePoint becomes a rich framework for portals, dashboards, records management, and other collaboration features. Although many people work with SharePoint content from their Web browsers, that's not the only way to interact with that content. You can use Outlook to work with shared calendars, contacts, and other SharePoint content; you can integrate that content into the application you probably use much of your day.

In environments in which Office Communications Server (OCS) is deployed and used for chat, desktop conferencing, and Voice over Internet Protocol (VoIP), Outlook can also integrate with Office Communicator, the client for OCS, to simplify communication. This chapter helps you understand and use the core features of SharePoint and OCS within Outlook 2010.

Adding SharePoint Calendars to Outlook

Outlook offers great features for managing your schedule. That it can display and even overlay multiple calendars is very handy for viewing schedules for multiple people or projects. If you use SharePoint to maintain shared calendars for time off, projects, team deliverables, and so on, you can open those calendars right in Outlook and work with them as if they were your own calendars in Outlook. Updates that you make in Outlook are synchronized to SharePoint, and vice versa. The first step is to connect the SharePoint calendar to Outlook.

Connect a SharePoint 2010 Calendar to Outlook

1. Open the SharePoint site and navigate to the calendar that you want to connect to Outlook.

2. Click the Calendar tab.

3. Click Connect To Outlook.

4. Click Allow.

5. Click Yes.

(continued on next page)

Tip

You must have Outlook 2007 or later to be able to create or edit SharePoint calendar items from Outlook.

Tip

To view details of an item in a SharePoint calendar, just click the item in SharePoint to open a form that shows those details.

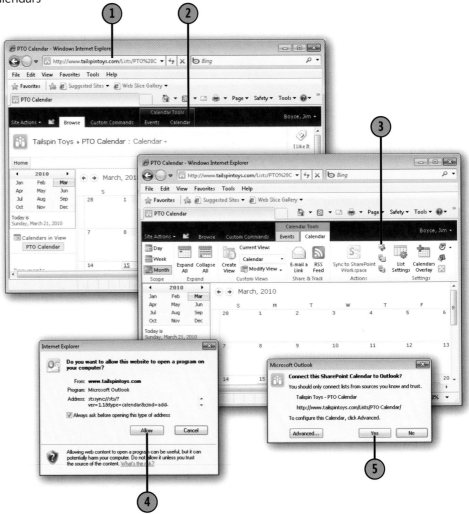

Connect a SharePoint 2010
Calendar to Outlook *(continued)*

6 Enter your credentials for the SharePoint site, if you're prompted.

7 Click OK.

8 The SharePoint calendar appears in Outlook.

9 The calendar appears in the Navigation Pane.

10 Click to overlay with your own calendar.

11 Outlook shows the overlaid calendars so that you can see combined calendar information.

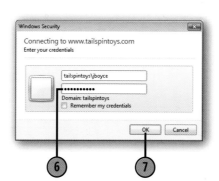

Tip Use Alerts to have SharePoint notify you when a calendar changes.

Tip Use RSS feeds to receive updates about calendar changes in your mailbox.

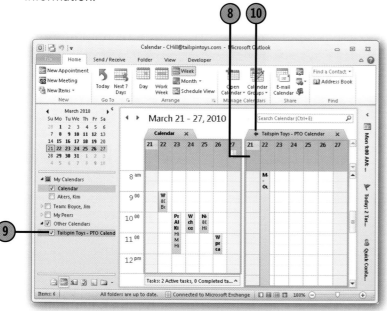

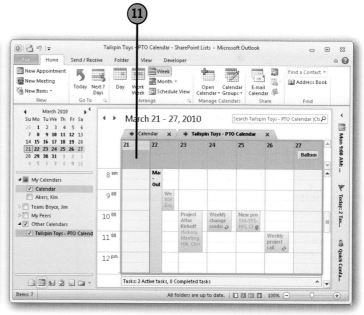

Connect a SharePoint 2007 Calendar to Outlook

1. Browse to the SharePoint calendar you want to connect to Outlook.

2. Click Actions and choose Connect To Outlook.

3. Click Allow.

4. Click Yes.

5. Enter your credentials for the SharePoint site, if you're prompted.

6. Click OK.

7. The calendar appears in Outlook.

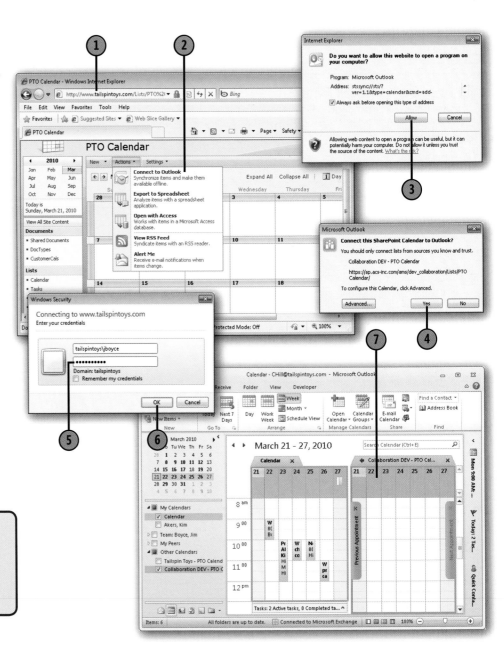

Tip

You can also use Outlook 2010 to interact with SharePoint 2007 and SharePoint 2010 calendars, as well as other types of lists in SharePoint.

Tip

You're not limited to making calendar changes from Outlook. You can open the SharePoint site, browse to the calendar, and if you have the right permissions, modify the calendar from your Web browser.

Create SharePoint Calendar Items in Outlook

After you have connected a SharePoint calendar to Outlook, you can work with that calendar in the same way you work with a local calendar in Outlook. You can create new items if you have the appropriate permissions in the SharePoint calendar, and you can edit existing items if you have the appropriate permissions for those items.

(1) Click the Calendar icon in Outlook to open the Calendar folder.

(2) Choose the SharePoint calendar you want to view.

(3) If you want, clear the check box for your default calendar to remove it from the view.

(4) Select a time range in the calendar.

(5) Click New Appointment.

(continued on next page)

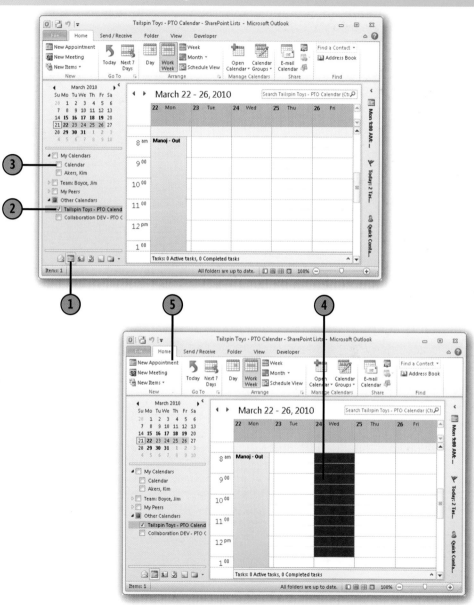

Create SharePoint Calendar Items in Outlook *(continued)*

6 Enter a subject for the calendar item, and then add other details if you need to.

7 Click the Save & Close button.

8 The new item appears in Outlook.

9 The new item also appears in SharePoint.

Tip

You can create meetings in a SharePoint calendar, but you won't receive a tally of responses from requested participants.

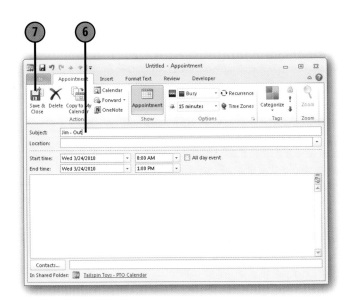

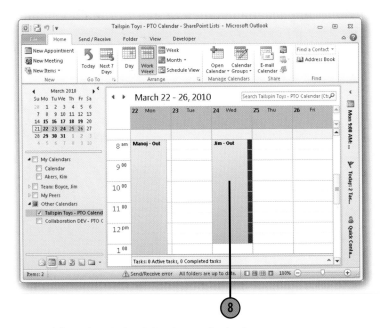

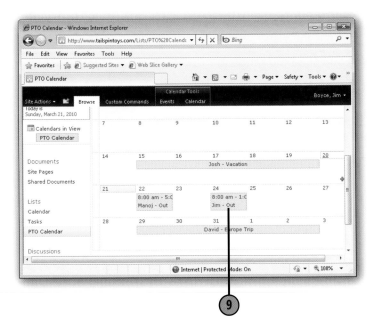

Using SharePoint Contacts in Outlook

If you use Exchange Server, your Global Address List (GAL) lists the people who have mailboxes in your organization and can also include other contacts added by the Exchange Server administrators. If you need to share other types of contacts—such as vendors or customers—with a team or even across your entire organization, you can turn to SharePoint as the place to share those contacts. Everyone can then connect that SharePoint contacts list in Outlook to work with the contacts, adding and updating them according to their SharePoint permissions for the shared list.

Connect a SharePoint 2010 Contact List to Outlook

Before you can use the SharePoint contact list in Outlook, you must connect it to Outlook, just as you do for a shared calendar or other list.

① Open the SharePoint site in your Web browser and navigate to the shared contacts list.

② Click the List tab.

③ Click Connect & Export, and then choose Connect to Outlook.

④ Click Allow.

⑤ Click Yes.

⑥ The shared contacts appear in Outlook.

⑦ The SharePoint list appears in the Navigation Pane.

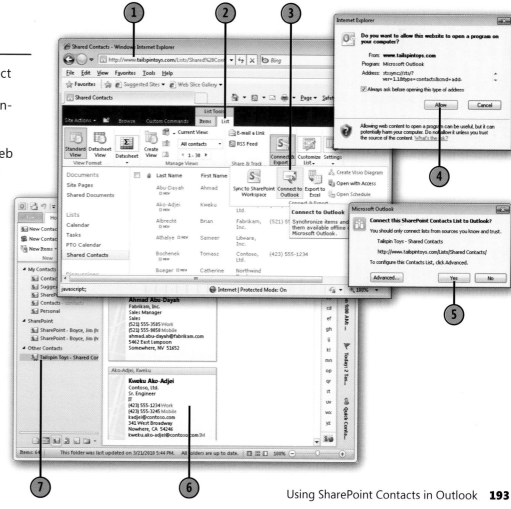

Create a Contact in a SharePoint List from Outlook

After you have connected a SharePoint contacts list to Outlook, you can add and modify contacts in the SharePoint list if you have the appropriate permissions in the list.

1. Click the SharePoint contact list in the Navigation Pane, and choose a different view, if you want.

2. Click New Contact in the New group on the Home tab of the ribbon.

3. Enter the name and other details for the new contact.

4. Click Save & Close.

(continued on next page)

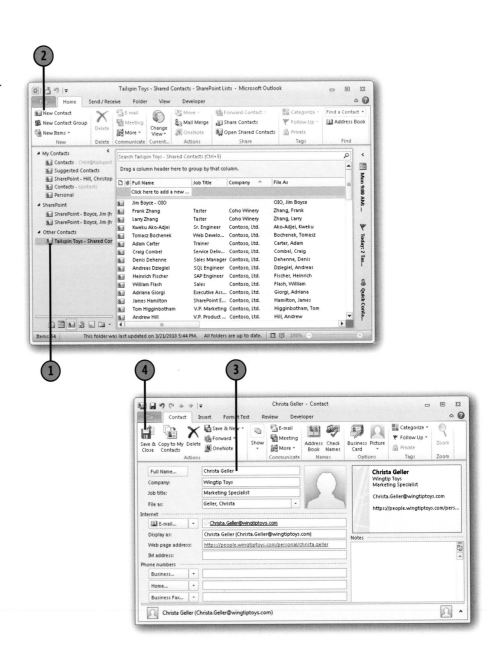

Create a Contact in a SharePoint List from Outlook *(continued)*

⑤ The new contact appears in the list in Outlook.

⑥ The new contact also appears in the SharePoint list.

Tip

It's relatively easy to copy your Outlook contacts to a SharePoint list to share them with others. Just create the shared contacts list in SharePoint, and then connect it to Outlook. Then simply copy the contacts from your Contacts folder to the SharePoint folder in Outlook.

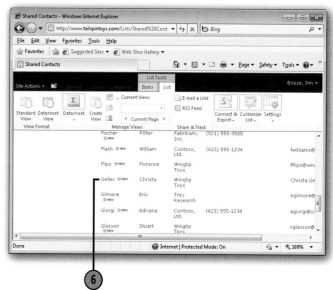

Using SharePoint Document Libraries in Outlook

SharePoint calendars and contacts are particular types of lists in SharePoint. You can connect other types of lists to Outlook, as well. For example, you can connect a document library to Outlook. When you do so, Outlook creates a cached local copy of the documents on your computer.

(1) Open the SharePoint document library that you want to connect to Outlook.

(2) Click the Library tab.

(3) Click Connect & Export, and then choose Connect To Outlook.

(4) Click Allow.

(5) Click Yes.

(continued on next page)

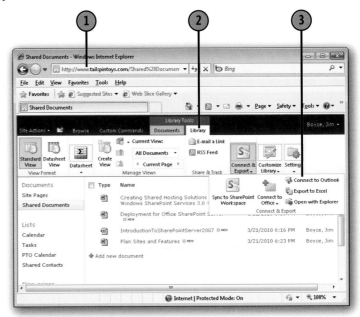

Tip

Connecting a SharePoint document library to Outlook creates a synchronized version of all of the documents in the library. If the library contains a large number of documents, or the documents themselves are large, it could take some time to download them to Outlook. It can also consume a large amount of local disk storage.

Using SharePoint Document Libraries in Outlook *(continued)*

⑥ Outlook performs a send/receive operation to synchronize the content from SharePoint to Outlook.

⑦ The documents appear in Outlook.

⑧ The Document Library appears in the Navigation Pane.

⑨ Preview the document in the Reading Pane.

⑩ Double-click a document to open it.

⑪ Click Edit Offline to edit the offline copy of the document. After you save your changes, Outlook synchronizes the updated copy to SharePoint.

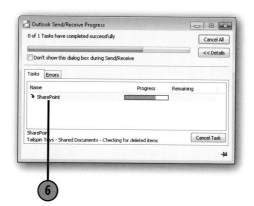

Tip

Consider SharePoint Workspace as an alternative to working with document libraries offline in Outlook—it enables you to work with SharePoint content offline without connecting the content in Outlook, and it gives you greater control over what is synchronized and when.

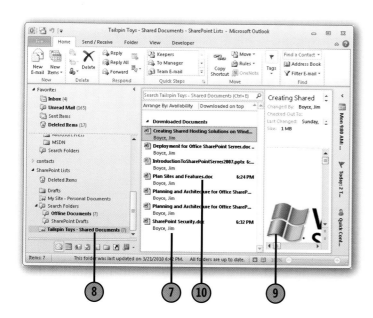

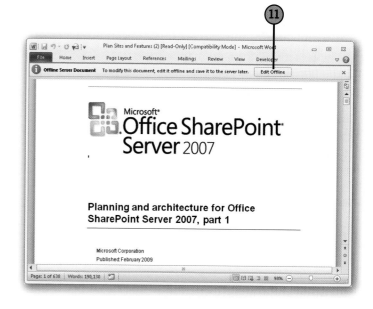

Using the People Pane

The People Pane in Outlook 2010 is a new feature that lets you view profile information, activities, and other information related to a particular person. Microsoft has developed an Outlook Social Connector for SharePoint, enabling the People Pane to display information from the person's profile data in SharePoint. Third-party developers can also create social connectors to work with Outlook, displaying information about the person from other social networking sites and services.

(1) Open Outlook and click the Mail icon to display the Inbox.

(2) Click the View tab.

(3) Click Reading Pane and choose either Right or Bottom.

(4) Click a message.

(5) Click to expand the People Pane.

(6) Click icons to view the various types of information associated with the e-mail's sender.

(7) The selected information appears in the People Pane.

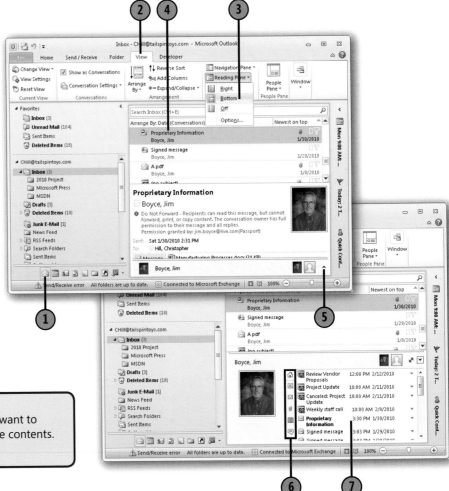

Tip

The People Pane appears at the bottom of the Reading Pane, so the Reading Pane must be turned on to use the People Pane.

Tip

You can minimize the People Pane when you don't want to take up more space in Outlook for the Reading Pane contents. You can also turn off the People Pane.

Viewing Online Status

Outlook 2010 lets you see online presence information about other users; it uses information from Office Communicator, Windows Live Messenger, MSN Messenger, or Windows Messenger. The presence information can tell you not only whether a person is online, but also whether he or she is available or busy. You can initiate a chat session or call or access other information about the user such as his or her SharePoint MySite.

Turn On Presence Display

Display of online presence is enabled by default in Outlook 2010, but you can turn it off—or on again if it has been turned off.

1. In Outlook, click the File tab.
2. Click Options.
3. Click Contacts.
4. Select Display Online Status Next To Name.
5. Click OK.

Tip

Clear the Show User Photographs When Available option if you don't want to see people's photos in the Reading Pane or People Pane.

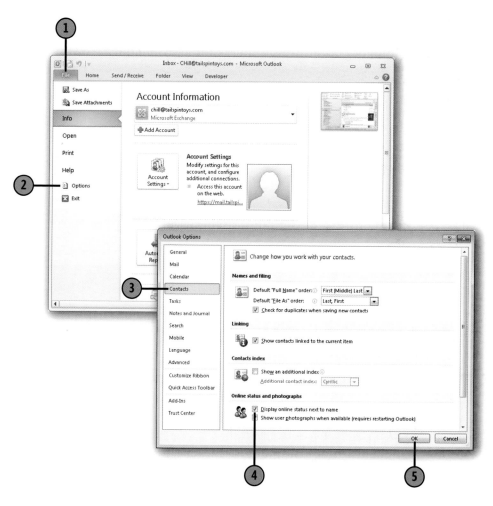

View Availability

After you have turned on presence display, you can view a person's availability in Outlook.

1. Open Outlook and click the Mail icon to show the Inbox.

2. Click a message to select it.

3. View the sender's online availability in the Reading Pane.

4. Double-click the message to open it.

5. Availability also appears in the message form.

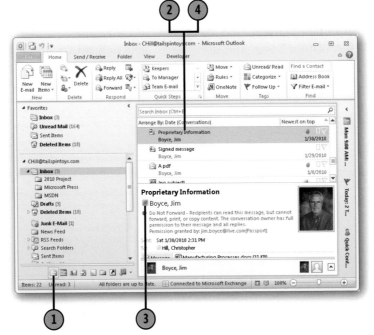

(2) (4)

(1) (3)

Tip

Outlook displays your own presence status beside your name, as well. For example, you can see what Office Communicator is showing as your current availability by looking beside your name in the address header of any message sent to you.

Tip

The indicator beside a person's name shows availability. Green indicates that person is available. Orange indicates that person is busy. Red with a white dash indicates Do Not Disturb. Yellow indicates that person is away.

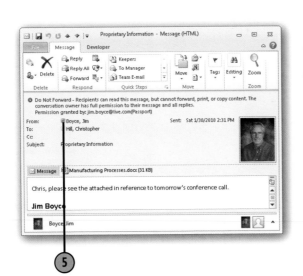

Indicates Do Not Disturb

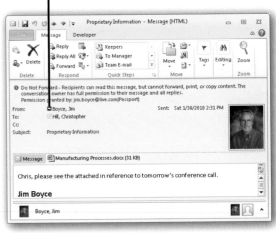

Communicating with Others from Outlook

Outlook isn't just for e-mail. It provides other features for communicating with coworkers and friends, particularly if you have Office Communicator or one of the other compatible instant messaging systems listed in the previous section. With presence information turned on, you can easily initiate a chat session or voice call with a contact. You can also send an e-mail or view the person's SharePoint MySite.

Start an Instant Messaging Session

Thanks to presence information, Outlook 2010 makes it very easy to start an instant messaging session with any of your online contacts. You only need to hover over the person's name and then click a button in the resulting pop-up window.

1. Open Outlook and click the Mail icon to open the Inbox.

2. Double-click a message to open it.

3. Hover the pointer over the person's name.

4. A pop-up window appears.

5. Click the Send an Instant Message button.

6. Your messaging application opens (Office Communicator, in this example).

7. Type a message and press Enter.

8. The other person receives the message and can respond.

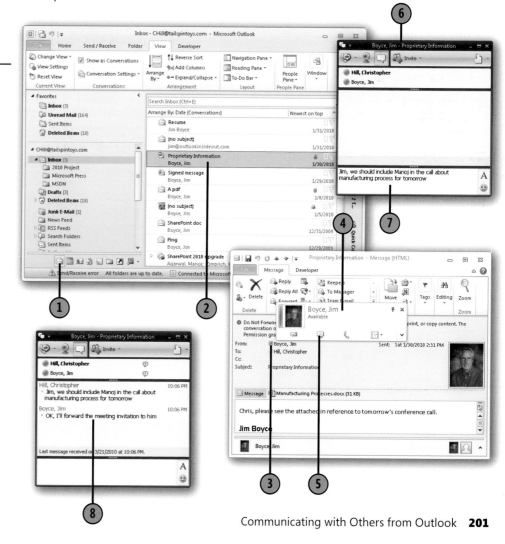

Start a Voice Call

If you have a microphone or VoIP phone, you can easily initiate a voice call using Outlook. Thanks to the presence information in Outlook, it only takes a couple of mouse clicks. You can start the call from the Contacts folder, but this example assumes you're starting it from a message in the Inbox.

1 Open the Inbox, and then open a message from the person you want to call.

2 Hover the pointer over the person's name.

3 In the pop-up window, click the Call button.

4 Office Communicator opens and initiates a call to the other person.

(continued on next page)

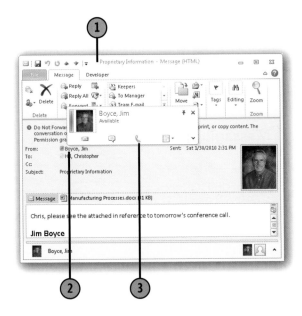

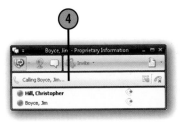

Start a Voice Call *(continued)*

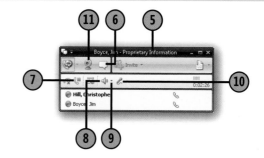

(5) After the other person answers, the Office Communicator window changes to offer other commands and options.

(6) Click to show the instant message area of the window.

(7) Click to put the call on hold.

(8) Click to mute the speakers.

(9) Click to change the volume.

(10) Click to mute your microphone.

(11) Click to start a video session.

(12) The other person's video, if they have a camera, appears in the Office Communicator window.

(13) A copy of your camera's output appears in an inset, or a picture of a webcam appears if you don't have a webcam or if it isn't configured or active.

(14) Click to end the call.

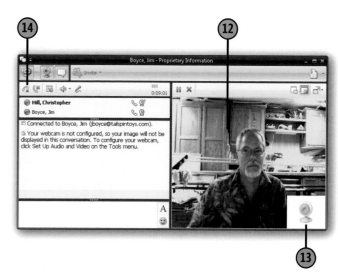

12

Managing Items and Folders

Microsoft Outlook 2010 gives you several ways to manage your Outlook items and folders, including organizing items in categories, creating and using folders to store items, and using the Mailbox Cleanup tool. For example, you can create folders to store e-mail messages relating to projects on which you work so that it's easier to locate those messages when you need them.

Categories feature lets you organize and sort your data in Outlook. You might assign a project category to all items for a specific project and then set up a view in each Outlook folder that displays the items grouped by category. This helps you quickly locate items associated with a specific project.

Outlook's abilities to help you manage messages threads (conversations) have improved also. You can group messages into conversations so you can view all messages in the thread, regardless of the folder in which they're stored. You can also use some new cleanup features to eliminate duplicate messages from a conversation.

Quick Steps are another new feature in Outlook 2010. Quick Steps are a little like rules except they don't have conditions. Instead, they're actions that you define and that you can apply to messages selectively.

Using Categories

Categories are colors with associated keywords or phrases that help you manage Outlook items such as contacts, e-mail messages, journal entries, and meetings. With categories, you can set up relationships between items stored in different places in Outlook. For example, you can categorize a piece of e-mail and a meeting reminder as business items. Then when you sort, filter, or search for all your business-related items, that e-mail message and meeting reminder appear.

Categorize an Item

① Select an item.

② Click Categorize on the Home tab of the ribbon.

③ Choose a category to assign to the item.

④ A category indicator appears in the Categories column and in the header.

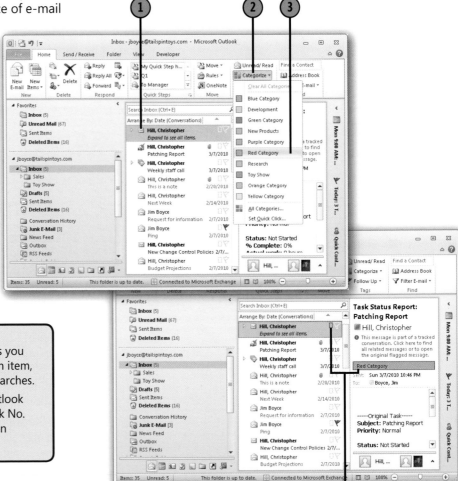

Tip ✓

You can associate an item with as many categories as you like. The more categories with which you associate an item, the easier it is to find that item when you conduct searches.

If this is the first time you have used the category, Outlook asks if you want to change the color. For now, just click No. You learn about changing category properties later in this section.

Assign Multiple Categories

1 Select an item.

2 Click Categorize on the Home tab of the ribbon.

3 Choose All Categories.

4 Select each category you want to assign.

5 Click OK.

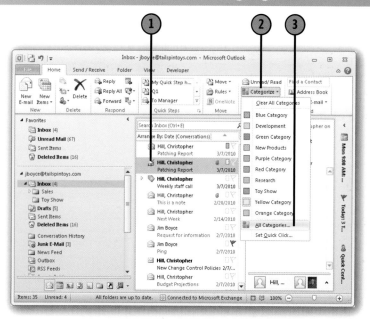

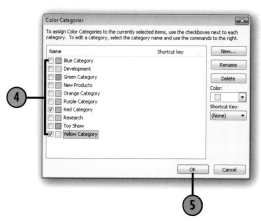

Add Categories to Your Category List

① Select an item.

② Click Categorize on the Home tab of the ribbon.

③ Choose All Categories.

④ Click New.

⑤ In the Add New Category dialog box that appears, type a new category name in the Name field.

⑥ Select a color.

⑦ Choose a shortcut key (if you want).

⑧ Click OK.

⑨ The new category appears in the Color Categories dialog box.

⑩ Deselect the check box if you want to create the category but not yet assign it.

⑪ Click OK.

Caution

If you assign a category to an item and then remove it from the Master Category list, the category isn't deleted from that item (or any others with that category assignment). You can still sort, view, or filter items based on deleted categories.

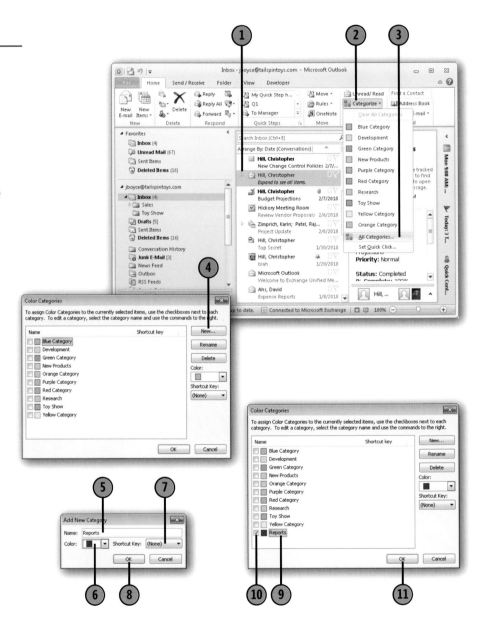

Rename a Category

1. Select an item.

2. Click Categorize on the Home tab of the ribbon.

3. Choose All Categories.

4. Click the category.

5. Click Rename.

6. Type a new name and press Enter.

7. Click OK

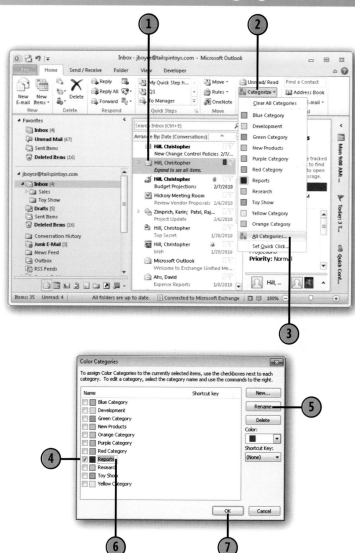

Delete a Category

① Select an item.

② Click Categorize on the Home tab of the ribbon.

③ Choose All Categories.

④ Click the category you want to delete.

⑤ Click Delete, and then click Yes when you're prompted to confirm the deletion.

⑥ Click OK.

Tip

Deleting a category that's in use only clears the color from the category. To remove the category altogether, you must clear the category from all items to which it's assigned.

Tip

If you want to clear a category from all items to which it's assigned, arrange the view by category. Locate the grouped category you want to remove, select all of the items in the group, right-click an item in the group, click Categorize, and click the category you want to remove.

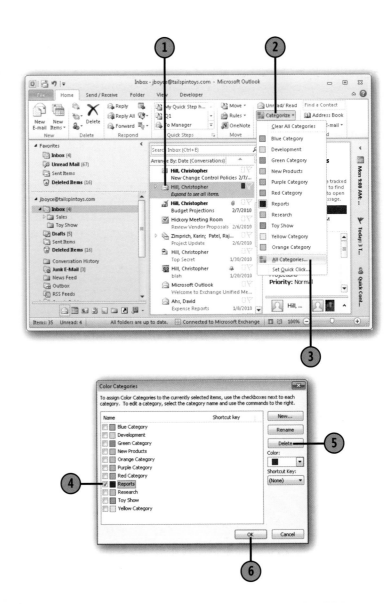

Using Search Folders

Search folders are a great feature that was added in Outlook 2003, and they have been made even better in subsequent versions. Search folders enable you to quickly locate messages anywhere they exist in your Outlook data store. Although a search folder looks and behaves like any other Outlook folder, the search folder is really a special way to display search results.

When you create the search folder, you specify the search conditions. Outlook then displays the results of the search in a folderlike way. However, the items that appear in the search folder actually reside in other locations—the search folder is just a way to group those messages together in one viewing location.

Use an Existing Search Folder

1 Click the Mail icon.

2 Click to expand the Search Folders branch.

3 Click Unread Mail.

4 All unread messages appear in the message pane.

5 Click Categorized Mail.

6 All messages that have category assignments appear in the message pane.

> **Tip**
>
> Outlook includes a handful of predefined search folders that you can use right away to locate unread messages, categorized messages, messages with attached faxes, and messages containing voice mail. Depending on your configuration, some of these might not be available to you.

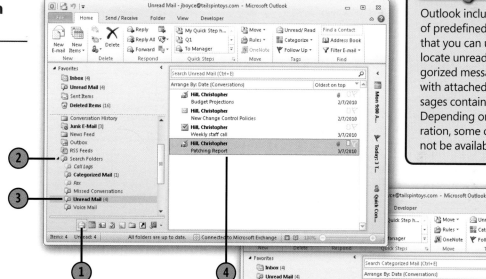

> **Tip**
>
> The figure to the right appears to show a message that isn't categorized. The item has a category assigned to it, but the category has been deleted from the master category list. If you see items in the Categorized Mail search folder that don't have a color associated with them, click the item, click Categorize, All Categories, and either clear the category or create and assign a new category to it.

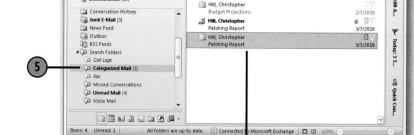

Create a Custom Search Folder

① Click the Mail icon in the Navigation Pane.

② Right-click Search Folders, and choose New Search Folder.

③ Scroll to the bottom of the list.

④ Choose Create A Custom Search Folder.

⑤ Click Choose.

⑥ Type a name for the search folder.

⑦ Click Criteria.

(continued on next page)

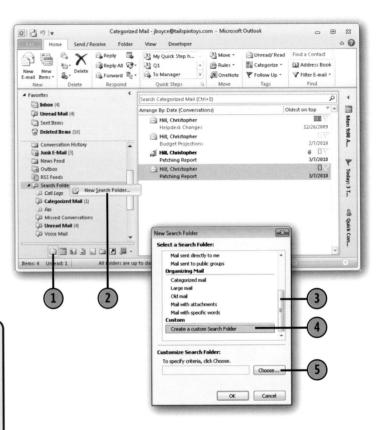

Tip

The Unread Mail search folder shows all unread messages, including those in folders other than the Inbox. Likewise, the Categorized Mail search folder shows all messages that have a category assigned from all folders in your mailbox. The Categorized Mail search folder doesn't show messages without a category assignment.

Tip

The options in the Search Folder Criteria dialog box give you a wide array of conditions to use in defining the search. For example, on the Messages tab, you can search for words or phrases, specify that the message is from a particular sender or sent to a particular recipient, and set a time frame in which the message was sent or received (as well as other time options).

Create a Custom Search
Folder *(continued)*

8 Click From and choose a contact, or type an e-mail address in the text box.

9 Click OK in the Search Folder Criteria dialog box.

10 Click OK in the Custom Search Folder dialog box.

11 Click OK in the New Search Folder dialog box.

12 Messages that fit the search condition appear in the message pane.

13 Click Inbox to view all messages in the Inbox.

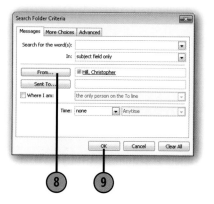

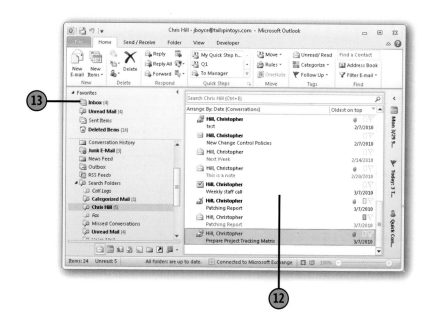

Modify a Search Folder

① Click the Mail icon on the Navigation Pane.

② Expand the Search Folders branch, if you need to.

③ Right-click the search folder you want to modify.

④ Choose Customize This Search Folder.

⑤ Change the name, if you want.

⑥ Click Criteria.

⑦ Click the More Choices tab.

⑧ Place a check mark beside Only Items With.

⑨ Choose One Or More Attachments.

⑩ Click OK in the Search Folders Criteria dialog box.

⑪ Click OK in the Customize dialog box.

⑫ The results of the new search criteria appear in the message pane.

Tip ✓

You can combine options on the More Choices tab to refine a search, such as searching for all messages with a specific category that have attachments and that are larger than a specified size (in KB). The choices on the Messages and More Choices tabs are naturally limited because of space. The Advanced tab lets you choose any of the message fields to include in the search criteria.

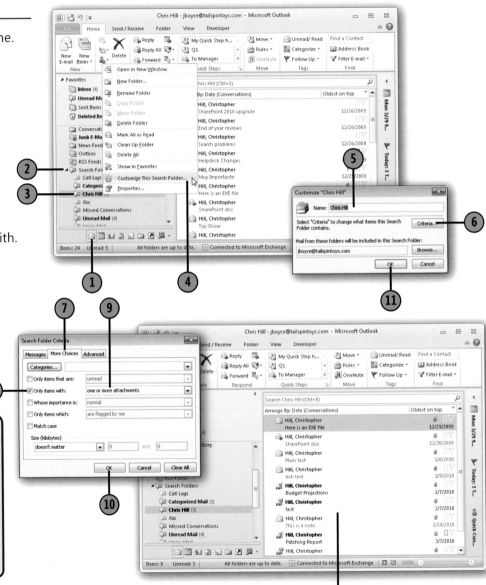

Organizing with Folders

Outlook 2010 uses folders to let you store items, such as e-mail messages and notes. Outlook folders are similar to the folders you can create and modify in Windows Explorer in that they help organize items. The Inbox folder, for example, is the default location for your incoming e-mail messages. The Outbox folder, on the other hand, stores your outgoing e-mail messages until you send them.

You can use the existing folders created automatically by Outlook, but you can also create your own folders to help you organize your items in a way that makes the most sense for the way you use Outlook.

Create a New Folder

1. In Outlook, click the Folder tab.

2. Click New Folder.

3. In the Create New Folder dialog box, type a new folder name in the Name text box.

4. Select the type of item that the folder is to contain from the Folder Contains drop-down list. For example, if you want a folder to store messages, select Mail And Post Items.

5. Select the location where you want the new folder to be placed.

6. Click OK.

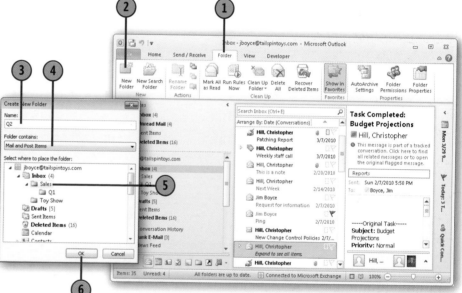

See Also

For information on Outlook folders, see "Exploring Outlook Folders" on page 33.

Tip ✓

You can create subfolders, which are folders within folders. Subfolders can help you manage your items in Outlook by letting you organize items in ways that help you do your work. For example, you can set up subfolders under a new folder you created for messages relating to various aspects of a project on which you're currently working. As you receive e-mail relating to those aspects, you can move the item from the Inbox to the appropriate subfolder.

Move Items to a Folder

(1) In the Outlook main window, choose the item you want to move.

(2) Click and drag the item from the message pane to the folder where you want to move the message.

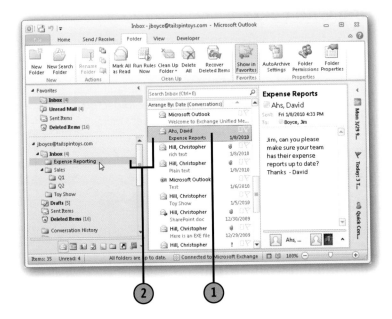

Move Items Without Dragging

① Select the message you want to move.

② Click Move on the Home tab of the ribbon and then choose the folder to which you want to move the item. Or if the folder isn't visible in the list, follow these steps:

③ Choose Other Folder.

④ In the Move Items dialog box that appears, click the target folder.

⑤ Click OK.

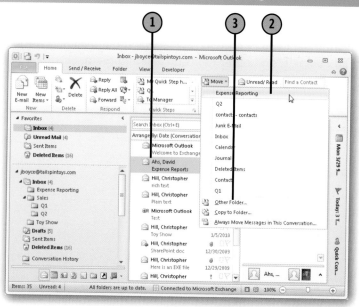

Try This!

If you move or copy an item, drag it while right-clicking instead of left-clicking. When you drop the item on a new folder, a short-cut menu appears. Choose Move, Copy, or Cancel to complete the operation.

Caution

Sometimes when you move an item, you might drop it into the wrong folder. If you do this, don't panic. Press Ctrl+Z immediately after you move the item. Outlook returns the item to its original location.

See Also

To learn how to move messages to other folders automatically by using rules, see "Working with the Rules Wizard" on page 86.

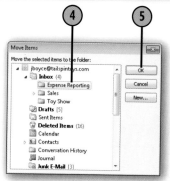

Cleaning Up Folders

You should get in the habit of cleaning out unwanted e-mail messages, old contacts, and other items by deleting them or moving them to other folders. Outlook 2010 provides the Mailbox Cleanup tool to help you manage your mailbox. This tool lets you reduce the size of your mailbox to increase Outlook's performance and make managing mailbox items easier.

Use the Mailbox Cleanup Tool

1 In Outlook, click the File tab.

2 Click Cleanup Tools, and then choose Mailbox Cleanup.

(continued on next page)

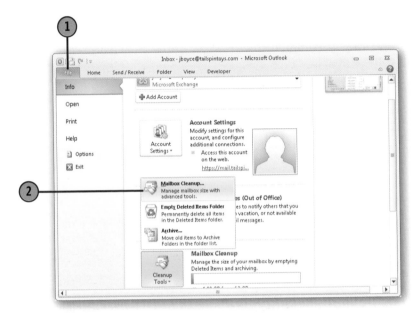

See Also

For information on setting AutoArchive options, see "Set the AutoArchive Options" on page 233.

Caution

Depending on the AutoArchive options set for a folder, messages older than a specific date may be removed from your current folders and placed in the Archive Folders. If you want to access a message that has been moved to these folders, open the folders from the Folder List pane and view the message in the main Outlook window.

Use the Mailbox Cleanup Tool *(continued)*

(3) In the Mailbox Cleanup dialog box that appears, click View Mailbox Size to display the Folder Size dialog box.

(4) View the size of your mailbox and other Outlook folders.

(5) Click Close to close the Folder Size dialog box, and return to the Mailbox Cleanup dialog box.

(6) Click AutoArchive to begin immediately archiving items based on the settings you have defined for Auto-Archive. The Mailbox Cleanup dialog box closes automatically while your mail is being archived.

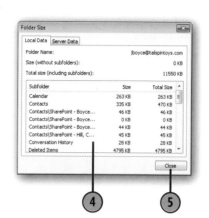

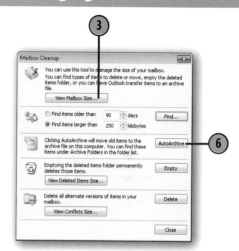

Tip

You can use the two search options in the Mailbox Cleanup dialog box to search for messages that are older than a specified length of time or that are larger than a specified size. In the resulting search results window, you can select items and delete them from your mailbox. To delete these items, first select them in the results pane, then right-click the items and choose Delete, or simply select the items and press the Delete key on the keyboard.

Tip

Click View Deleted Items Size to view the amount of space taken up by your Deleted Items folder. Click Empty to permanently delete all items in the Deleted Items folder.

Deleting Items

Over time, your Outlook folders fill up and can seem unmanageable. Outlook allows you to delete items when you no longer need them. When you delete an item, the program removes it from its current folder and places it in the Deleted Items folder.

Delete an Item

① In an Outlook folder, choose the item you want to delete.

② Click Delete on the toolbar.

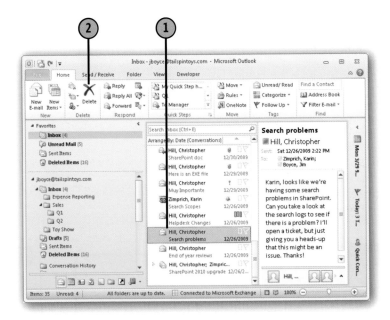

Empty the Deleted Items Folder

1. In the Navigation Pane, right-click the Deleted Items folder.

2. Choose Empty Folder.

3. Click Yes to empty the Deleted Items folder.

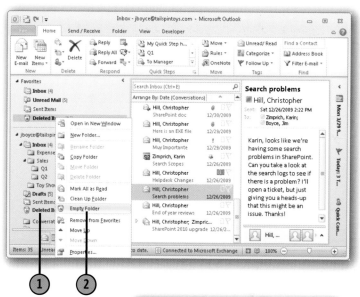

Try This!

To set up Outlook to empty the Deleted Items folder when you exit Outlook, click Options in the File menu. Click Advanced, and then select Empty Deleted Items Folders Exiting Outlook. Click OK.

See Also

For information on managing the Inbox Folder, including deleting unneeded messages, see "Managing the Inbox Folder" on page 76.

Caution

If you configure Outlook to empty the Deleted Items folder when you exit, keep in mind that all items in the Deleted Items folder are permanently deleted when you exit Outlook. They're no longer available in the Deleted Items Folder the next time you start Outlook.

13

Managing Your Outlook Files

Microsoft Outlook 2010 stores your data in special types of files called *Outlook data files*. The main type of file is a personal folder file, or PST file. Outlook can store a complete set of Outlook folders—in addition to custom folders you add—in a PST file. For example, a particular PST would include Calendar, Inbox, and Tasks folders, along with custom folders.

In addition to storing data in PST files, Outlook can store data in a Microsoft Exchange Server mailbox. The mailbox resides on the server rather than on your computer. When you open Outlook, the program contacts the server to display your data.

Sometimes your computer can't communicate with the server because the server is offline or because you may be working on a computer that isn't connected to the network. In these situations, Outlook can use a set of offline folders stored in an offline folder file, or OST file. Outlook stores data in the OST file and synchronizes the changes with the mailbox the next time it is able to connect to the server.

This section explains how to perform several tasks with your Outlook data files, including how to add new data files, use an existing file, and import and export items. The section also explains how to back up and restore your Outlook data in a PST file and how to archive items.

Working with Outlook Data Files

Unless your only e-mail account is on an Exchange Server, Outlook creates a local data file for you when you set up your Outlook profile. When Exchange Server is the only account, Outlook stores all items in your Exchange Server mailbox. You can easily create a new PST file and then add or remove folders to it as needed.

Create a New Data File

1 In Outlook, click the File tab.

2 Click the Account Settings button, and choose the Account Settings option.

3 View the existing data files, if any, on the Data Files tab.

4 Click Add to open the Create Or Open Outlook Data File dialog box.

(continued on next page)

See Also

For more information on working with Outlook folders, see "Exploring Outlook Folders" on page 33.

Tip

When you add an Exchange Server account to an Outlook 2010 profile, Outlook automatically sets up the account for Cached Exchange Mode, which makes a local copy of your mailbox. Items are still stored on the server, even though Outlook also keeps a cached local copy.

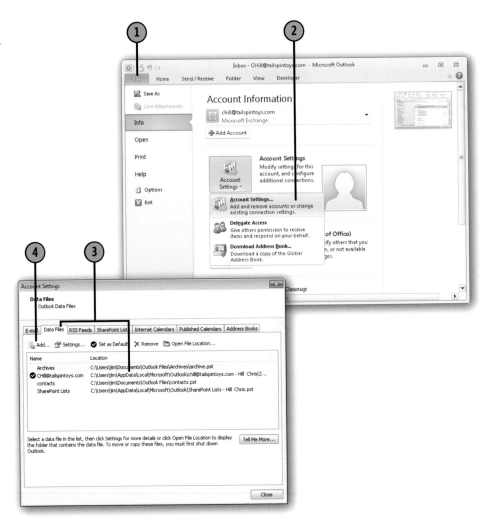

Create a New Data File   *(continued)*

(5) Browse for the location you want (if other than the default location).

(6) Type a name for the PST file.

(7) Click OK.

(8) The new file appears in the Data Files tab.

(9) Click Close.

(10) The new set of folders appears in your folder list.

Try This!

You can easily add folders to your new set of personal folders. Open Outlook, right-click in the folder list, and choose New Folder. Select a location in the new folder set, specify a name for the new folder, select the folder type, and click OK to create the new folder.

Tip

You can select an existing PST file in the Create Or Open Outlook Data File dialog box rather than create a new one. This method is good for moving a PST file from one computer to another. To accomplish that feat, copy the PST to the new computer, open Outlook, and add the existing PST to your profile. You are then able to access all of the items in the old PST.

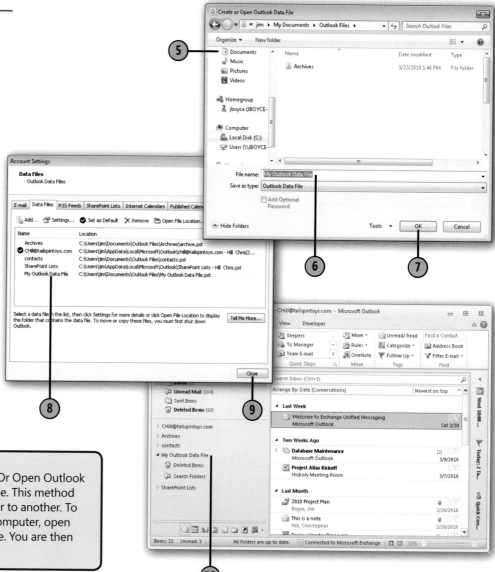

Importing and Exporting Items

Although you probably do much of your work in Outlook, occasionally you might want to move data into Outlook from other programs or export data from Outlook to another program.

Outlook makes it easy to import and export items. This section focuses on how to import and export items to and from PST files.

Import Items into Outlook

1. Click the File tab.
2. Click Open.
3. Click Import.
4. Select Import From Another Program Or File.
5. Click Next.
6. Select Outlook Data File.
7. Click Next.

(continued on next page)

See Also

For more information on importing other types of data, see "Importing Data from Another Program" on page 40.

Tip

You can use the import feature in Outlook to import messages and other items from other PST files, bring contacts from an Access database or Excel spreadsheet to your Contacts folder, and move other types of information from their original locations to other folders.

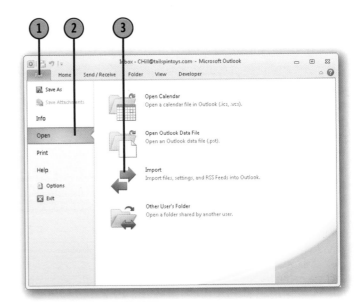

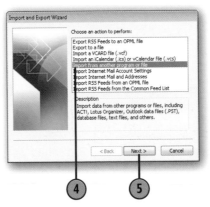

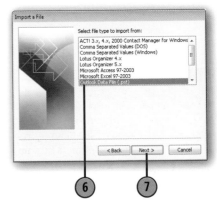

Import Items into Outlook *(continued)*

(8) Click Browse to locate the PST file from which you want to import.

(9) Select an option to specify how you want duplicate items to be handled.

(10) Click Next.

(11) Select the folder from which you want to import items.

(12) Click Filter to open the Filter dialog box.

(13) Specify options that define (filter) the data that Outlook will import.

(14) Click OK

(15) Click Finish.

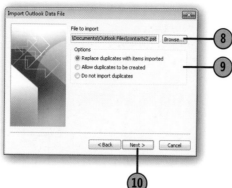

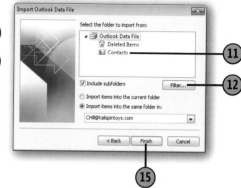

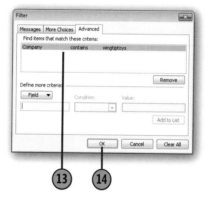

Tip

You can use the Filter dialog box to selectively import items. For example, perhaps you want to import only items that have the category Personal assigned to them. Or maybe you want to import only messages that came from specific senders or only contacts that work for a particular company. Whatever the case, the Filter dialog box lets you control which items are imported.

Tip

Importing selected items from a PST file gives you an easy way to selectively copy Outlook items from one computer to another. Simply copy the PST file from the source computer to the destination computer, and then use the Import feature to import only those items you want on the destination computer.

Export Items from Outlook

① Click the File tab, click Open, and click Import.

② Select Export To A File.

③ Click Next.

④ Select Outlook Data File (.pst).

⑤ Click Next.

(continued on next page)

Tip

You don't have to export to a new PST file. You can export items to an existing PST file. This method gives you a handy means of selectively backing up or archiving specific items. For example, you might back up selected items from your Exchange Server mailbox to a PST file on your local computer for safekeeping.

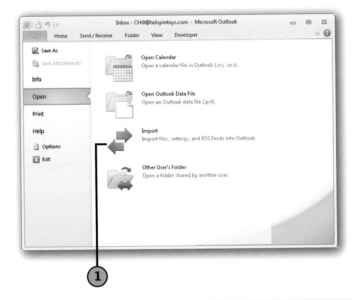

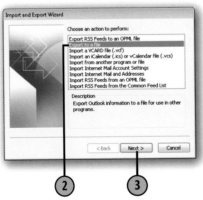

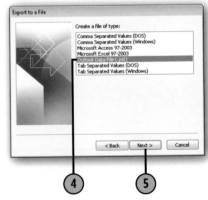

Export Items from Outlook *(continued)*

⑥ Select the folder from which you want to export items.

⑦ Click Filter to open the Filter dialog box.

⑧ Specify options that control (filter) the data that Outlook will import, such as in this example of items received in the last seven days.

⑨ Click OK

⑩ Click Next.

⑪ Specify the path and name of the file to which you want to export, or click Browse to select a file.

⑫ Specify how you want duplicate items to be handled.

⑬ Click Finish.

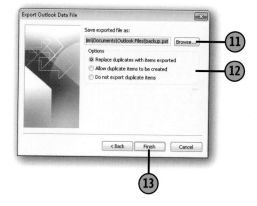

See Also

For more information on creating and using Outlook files, see "Working with Outlook Data Files" on page 224.

Tip

If you specify a file in step 11 that doesn't exist, Outlook displays the Create Outlook Data File dialog box after you click Finish. Simply click OK to create the file and complete the export process.

Backing Up and Restoring a Data File

If you use a set of personal folders in a PST file as your only data store or in addition to an Exchange Server mailbox, back up that PST file so that your data is still available if your computer experiences a problem such as a failed hard drive. Having the PST file backed up allows you to restore the file and recover your data.

Back Up Outlook Data

① On the File tab, click the Account Settings button, and then click the Account Settings option that appears.

(continued on next page)

Caution

Don't back up your PST file to the hard drive it's currently on. If that drive fails, you lose both copies of the file. Instead, back up the file to another hard drive, if your computer has more than one, or to another backup disk, CD, or flash drive.

Tip

Set up a regular backup schedule for your PST file, and make sure you back it up frequently to avoid losing any data.

Back Up Outlook Data   *(continued)*

② Click the Data Files tab, and then double-click the folder you want to back up to open the Personal Folders dialog box for the file.

③ Click in the Filename field, and use the arrow keys on the key-board to view the whole path for the file. Make note of the file name and location.

④ Click OK.

⑤ Click Close, and then close Outlook. You can now locate the file on your hard drive and manually create and store a backup copy in a safe location.

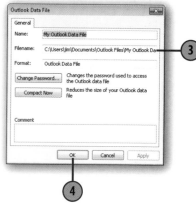

Caution

Make sure you close Outlook before making a backup copy of your PST file.

Tip

You can use a backup program to back up the PST file if you don't want to copy it manually or if you need to copy it to tape or CD-R/CD-RW. All versions of Windows include a Backup program in the Accessories menu that you can use to back up the file. CD-R and CD-RW drives usually include software you can use to copy files to a CD. The advantage of using a backup program to back up your PST file is that the backup program keeps track of the file's original location and restores the file to that location by default. This saves you the trouble of trying to remember the file's original location.

Restore Outlook Data

1. Close Outlook, and then use Computer (My Computer in Windows XP and earlier) or Libraries in Windows 7 to open the folder containing the backup file.

2. Click the file you want to restore.

3. Right-click the file and choose Copy.

4. Open the original location for the file. This location is the one recorded in the Personal Folders dialog box for the file, as described in the previous procedure.

5. Right-click and choose Paste.

6. Open Outlook, and verify that your data items are intact.

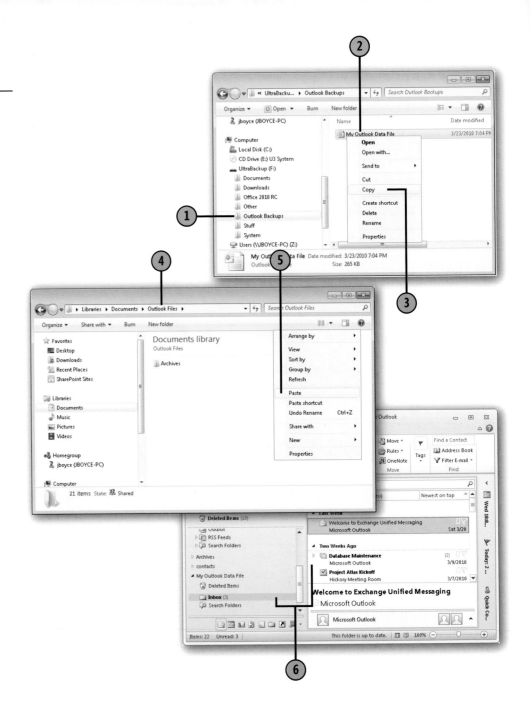

Archiving Outlook Data Files

Old messages, tasks, and other items have a tendency to pile up unless you clean them out. Outlook provides an AutoArchive feature that lets you specify how often Outlook should clean out old items, where it should place those items (or whether it should delete them), which items to move, and so on. If you choose to archive items rather than delete them, Outlook places them in a PST file of your choosing. You can then recover them by opening that set of folders and copying the items back to your regular folders or by using the Import feature in Outlook to import from the archive file.

Set the AutoArchive Options

① Click the File tab, and then click Options to display the Outlook Options dialog box.

② Click Advanced in the left pane.

③ Click AutoArchive Settings to open the AutoArchive dialog box.

④ Select the options that will control the AutoArchive function, including its frequency, how old messages should be before they are archived, and whether items should be moved to another folder.

⑤ Click to set archive options for all folders according to the settings in the dialog box.

⑥ Click OK.

⑦ Click OK to close the Options dialog box.

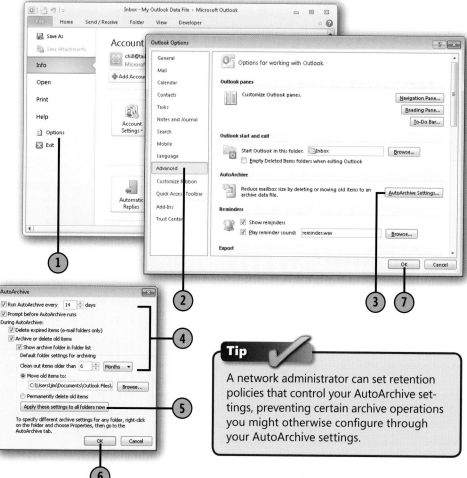

Caution

Select the Prompt Before AutoArchive Runs option if you want to be able to control whether Outlook archives items. If this option isn't selected, Outlook performs the archive operation without warning you.

Tip

A network administrator can set retention policies that control your AutoArchive settings, preventing certain archive operations you might otherwise configure through your AutoArchive settings.

Archive to an Outlook Data File

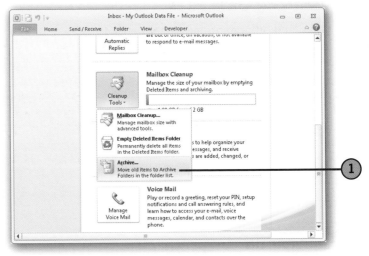

① Click the File tab, scroll down, click Cleanup Tools, and choose Archive.

② Select this option if you want to archive all folders using the AutoArchive settings.

③ Select this option if you want to archive only the selected folder and its subfolders.

④ Select the folder from which you want to archive items.

⑤ Specify how old items must be to be archived.

⑥ Select this option to archive items that would otherwise be skipped because you have configured them not to AutoArchive.

⑦ Select the file in which you want to store the archived items.

⑧ Click OK to archive the items.

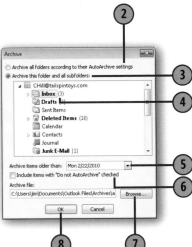

Tip

Back up your archive file each time you back up your PST file to make sure you can recover archived items if a system or drive failure causes you to lose your regular archive file.

See Also

For more information on backing up PST files, see "Backing Up and Restoring a Data File" on page 230.

Try This!

Test your ability to recover archived items. Open the AutoArchive dialog box, and note the location of your archive file. Review the "Import Items into Outlook" task earlier in this chapter, and import a selection of items from your archive PST file.

Working with Offline Folders

When you use an Exchange Server mailbox, Outlook stores your data in the mailbox. As long as the server is available, you can access your data. If the server is offline or you're not connected to the network, you can't continue working with your mailbox data unless you configure a set of offline folders and set Outlook to use Cached Exchange Mode. In this mode, Outlook uses the offline folders as a temporary storage location

for your data until you can connect to the server once again. Then Outlook synchronizes any changes between the mailbox and the offline folders.

By default, Outlook configures an Exchange Server account to use Cached Exchange Mode. However, if you turn it off or an administrator preconfigures a profile for you without Cached Exchange Mode, you can enable it on an existing account.

Configure Outlook for Cached Exchange Mode

1. Click the File tab, click the Account Settings button, and choose the Account Settings option.

2. In the Account Settings dialog box that appears, click the Exchange Server account on the E-mail tab.

3. Click Change.

(continued on next page)

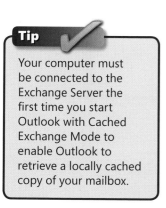

Tip

Your computer must be connected to the Exchange Server the first time you start Outlook with Cached Exchange Mode to enable Outlook to retrieve a locally cached copy of your mailbox.

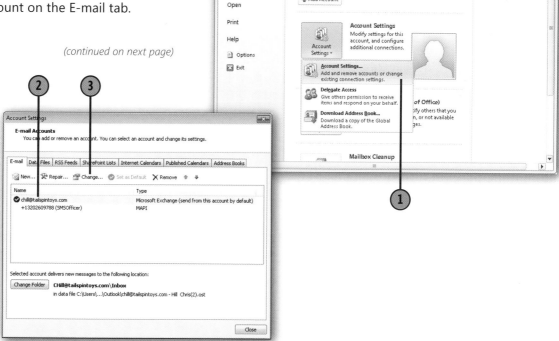

Configure Outlook for Cached Exchange Mode   *(continued)*

④ Select the Use Cached Exchange Mode option.

⑤ Click Next.

⑥ Click Finish.

⑦ Close and restart Outlook.

Tip

Outlook 2010 automatically synchronizes your folders when using Cached Exchange Mode. It detects when the server is available and then synchronizes your folders for you in the background.

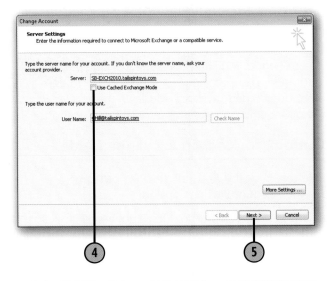

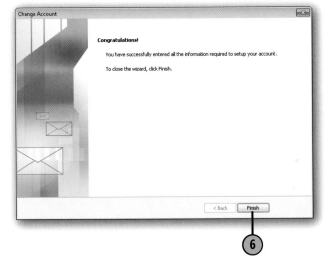

14

Customizing Outlook

Although Microsoft Outlook 2010 can be used out of the box, one of its finest features is its ability to be customized to look and work the way you work. You can customize Outlook in a number of ways. You can choose formats to customize outgoing mail messages. Using Calendar, you can set up holiday schedules to match those recognized by your business or organization and specify your workweek. For example, if your workweek differs from the traditional 8:00 A.M. to 5:00 P.M., Monday through Friday, you can change Outlook's Calendar views to match the days and hours you work, at least in most cases.

You also can specify how Contact items are sorted. Finally, you can customize Outlook's toolbars and the Navigation Pane.

Using Read and Delivery Receipts

Outlook can help you manage your e-mail messages by keeping track of when messages that you send are delivered and read by their recipients. This is handy when you send a time-sensitive e-mail and you want to know when the recipients received and read the message.

Use Read and Delivery Receipts on Individual Messages

1. Open the Inbox, and click New E-mail on the Home tab of the ribbon to start a new e-mail message.

2. Click the Options tab on the ribbon.

3. Select the Request A Delivery Receipt option.

4. Select the Request A Read Receipt option.

5. Click Send to send the message as you normally would. Outlook sends you a delivery receipt when the message is delivered to the user's mailbox (although not all mail servers send delivery receipts).

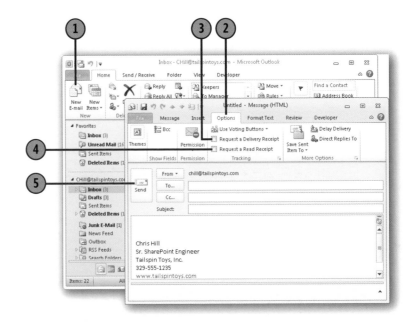

Tip

In the Properties dialog box for the message, you can set priority levels for an e-mail message. Click the Importance drop-down list, and select Low, Normal, or High. Low or High importance messages are sent at the same speed as Normal, but the recipient sees a symbol that indicates the importance of the message.

Try This!

To set Outlook so that all messages have a delivery and read receipt, click File, Options and click Mail. Scroll down to the Tracking group, and select Read Receipt Confirming The Recipient Viewed The Message and Delivery Receipt Confirming The Message Was Delivered To The Recipient's E-mail Server.

Choosing Message Formats

When you create new e-mail messages, you can specify the format in which the message should be created. The format you choose must be supported by the e-mail program used by the recipient of the message. Outlook also allows you to set up your environment so that all your messages use the same format. You can choose from Plain Text, Rich Text, or HTML as the default.

Select a Format for the Open Message

① Create a new message.

② Click the Format Text tab on the ribbon.

③ Choose a format from the Format group:

- Choose Plain Text to create a message without formatting.

- Choose HTML to create a message with HTML support, such as embedded tables, inserted pictures, and live hyperlinks.

- Choose Rich Text to create a message with rich text formatting support, such as embedded objects, font specifications, and colored text.

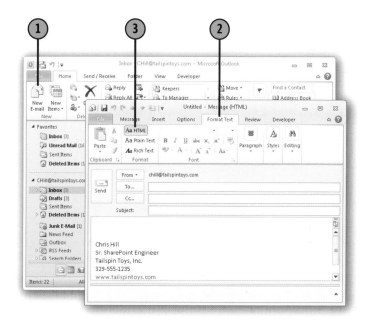

Tip ✓

If you aren't sure of the format that your recipient can read, use the Plain Text option. This ensures nothing is lost in the translation if your recipient's e-mail program doesn't support Rich Text or HTML messages.

See Also

For information on using Rich Text or HTML message formats, see "Formatting Message Text" on page 57.

Select a Default Message Format

(1) Click the File tab, and then Options.

(2) Click Mail in the left pane.

(3) Click the Compose Messages In This Format drop-down list, and choose the format you want to use for all your messages.

(4) Click OK.

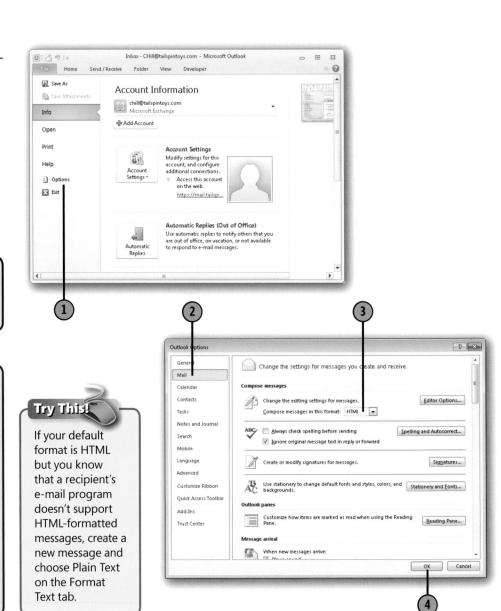

See Also

For more on formatting information in your messages, see "Add Formatting to a Message" on page 58.

Tip

When you use HTML formatting, your messages can include pictures that are located on the Internet. If you want to embed a picture instead of creating a hyperlink to it (which would require the recipients to have an Internet connection to view the picture), click Picture in the Illustrations group of the ribbon's Insert tab. In the Insert Picture dialog box, click in the filename field and type the picture's URL (something like *http://www.boyce.us/images/jim.jpg*). Then click the down arrow beside the Insert button, and choose Insert and Link. Outlook retrieves a copy of the image and embeds it in the message.

Try This!

If your default format is HTML but you know that a recipient's e-mail program doesn't support HTML-formatted messages, create a new message and choose Plain Text on the Format Text tab.

Setting Calendar Options

Outlook enables you to change the way Calendar works. You can change the default Monday through Friday work week to one that is specific to your schedule (perhaps you work Wednesday through Saturday). You also can set up holidays that aren't traditionally observed in the United States.

Set the Work Week

① Click the File tab, and then Options.

② Click Calendar on the left pane.

③ Select the days of the week that you work.

④ Click the Start Time drop-down list, and select the time your workday begins.

⑤ Do the same in the End Time list for the end of your workday.

⑥ Click OK.

Tip ✓

You can specify which day of the week is the first day for you. Click the First Day Of Week drop-down list, and click a day.

Try This! 🖱

Change your work hours to begin at 12:00 A.M. and end at 7:00 A.M. Click the Calendar icon on the Navigation Pane and click the Day button on the Home tab of the ribbon. Notice how the 12–7 range is shown in white to indicate your workday hours. Also, note that you cannot specify a start time from the previous day. For example, if your work "day" runs from 11:00 P.M. to 7:00 A.M. the next morning, you can't specify those start and end times. Instead, you would have to specify 12:00 A.M. as your start time.

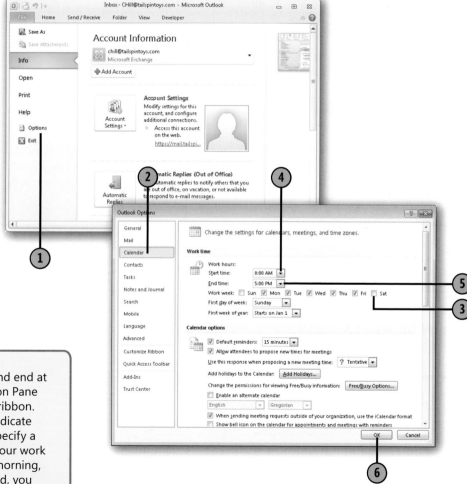

Add Holidays

1. Click the File tab, and then Options.
2. Click Calendar on the left pane.
3. Click Add Holidays.
4. Select the country or holiday set that includes the holidays you want to add to your Calendar.
5. Click OK in the Add Holidays to Calendar dialog box.
6. Click OK in the Outlook Options dialog box.

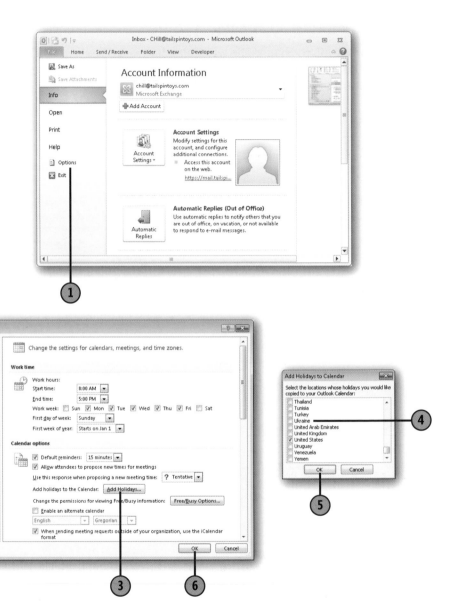

Tip

If you want to add a nontraditional holiday to Calendar, set it up as an event in your Calendar folder.

See Also

For information on adding events to Calendar, see "Adding an Appointment" on page 129 and "Adding an Event" on page 132.

Customizing the Navigation Pane

The Navigation Pane includes icons you click to quickly open an Outlook folder. You can customize the Navigation Pane in several ways, such as by turning it off when you want more room to see items in Outlook or by adding a shortcut group to the icons displayed in the bar.

Show or Hide the Navigation Pane

① Click the Minimize the Navigation Pane button.

② The Navigation Pane minimizes.

③ Click the Expand the Navigation Pane button to expand the Navigation Pane again.

Tip ✓

You also can hide the Navigation Pane by choosing Navigation Pane from the View tab of the ribbon and then choosing Minimized.

Tip ✓

Minimize the Navigation Pane by clicking the left-pointing arrow at the upper-right corner of the Navigation Pane.

See Also

To learn more about the Navigation Pane, see "Exploring Outlook Folders" on page 33.

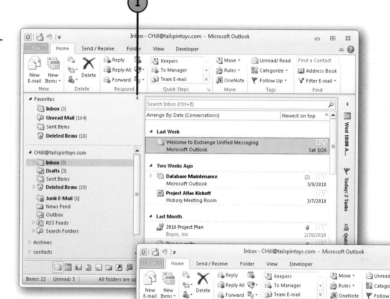

Add a Shortcut Group to the Navigation Pane

① Click the Shortcuts button on the Navigation Pane.

② Outlook displays the Shortcuts pane.

③ Right-click Shortcuts

④ Choose New Shortcut.

⑤ Choose the Outlook folder for which you want to create a shortcut.

⑥ Click OK.

(continued)

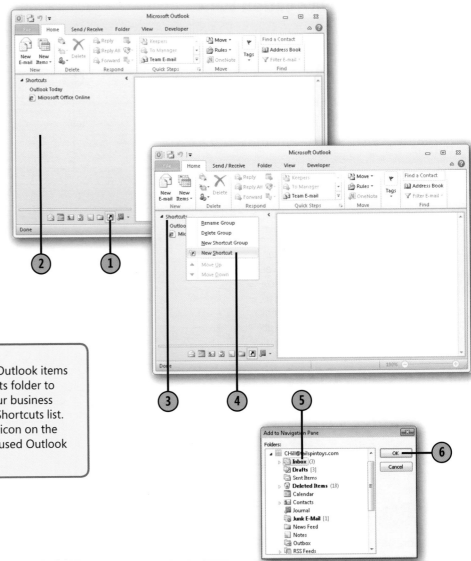

Try This!

Add several shortcut groups to help you access Outlook items you use often. For example, create a new contacts folder to store your personal contacts separately from your business contacts. Create a shortcut to that folder in the Shortcuts list. When you want to open that folder, just click its icon on the shortcut group. Add all of your most frequently used Outlook folders to the list.

Add a Shortcut Group to the Navigation Pane *(continued)*

⑦ The folder shortcut appears in the Shortcuts list.

⑧ Right-click Shortcuts

⑨ Click New Shortcut Group.

⑩ Outlook adds a new group.

⑪ Type a new name for the group and press Enter.

Tip

You can add shortcuts to your favorite Web sites on the Shortcuts list. Just create a shortcut on the Windows desktop to the Web site, and then drag the shortcut to the Shortcuts list in the Navigation Pane. You need to drop the shortcut icon right on the Shortcuts or a group header for this to work correctly.

Tip

When you add a shortcut for a Web site to the Shortcuts pane, the Web site opens within Outlook, not in your Web browser.

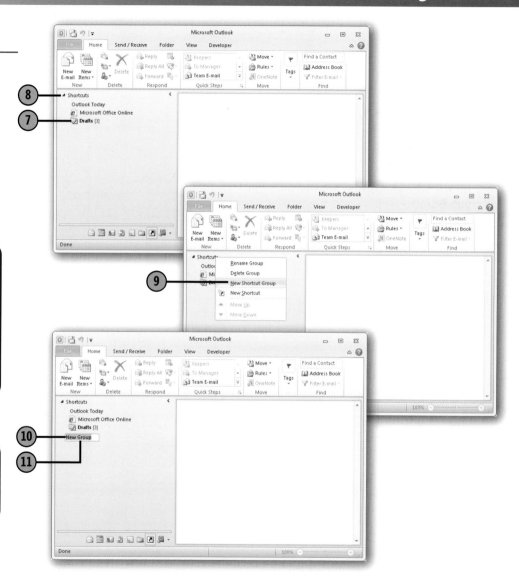

Drag Items to Create Shortcuts

① Click the Folder button to open the folder list.

② Drag an item to the Shortcuts button, and hold it there without releasing the mouse button.

③ The Shortcuts pane opens.

④ Continue to drag the folder and drop it on the shortcut group header that you want.

⑤ Outlook creates a shortcut to the item.

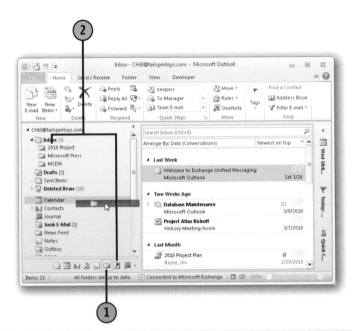

Add Shortcuts to Non-Outlook Items

① In the Start menu or Windows Explorer, find a program for which you want to create a shortcut.

② Right-click the program, and choose Send To.

③ Click Desktop (Create Shortcut).

④ Windows creates a shortcut on the Windows desktop.

⑤ Open Outlook and position it so that you can see the shortcut on the desktop.

⑥ Click the Shortcuts button to open the Shortcuts pane.

⑦ Drag the shortcut from the desktop to the target shortcut group header.

⑧ Outlook adds the shortcut to the group.

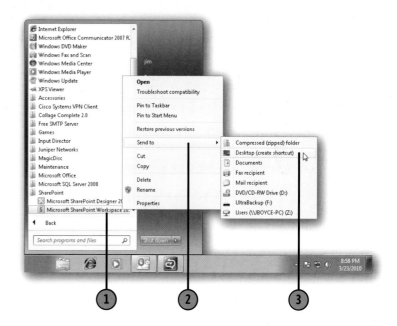

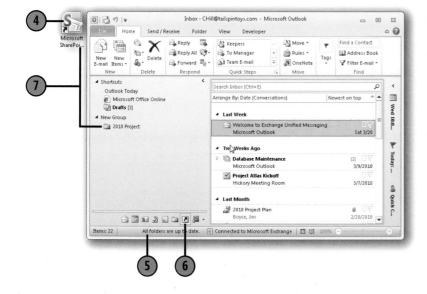

Customizing the Outlook Ribbon

The ribbon, which appeared only in certain forms in Outlook 2007, is now used throughout the Outlook 2010 interface. While the ribbon gives you quick access to frequently used commands in a very organized way, it also lets you change the ribbon to suit your needs. For example, you might want to add your own tab of favorite commands so you don't have to switch back and forth between tabs. You can also turn tabs on or off altogether.

Turn Tabs On or Off

① In Outlook, right-click any tab on the ribbon and choose Customize The Ribbon.

② Scroll down until you locate Developer in the list, and then select it.

③ Click OK.

④ The tab appears in the ribbon.

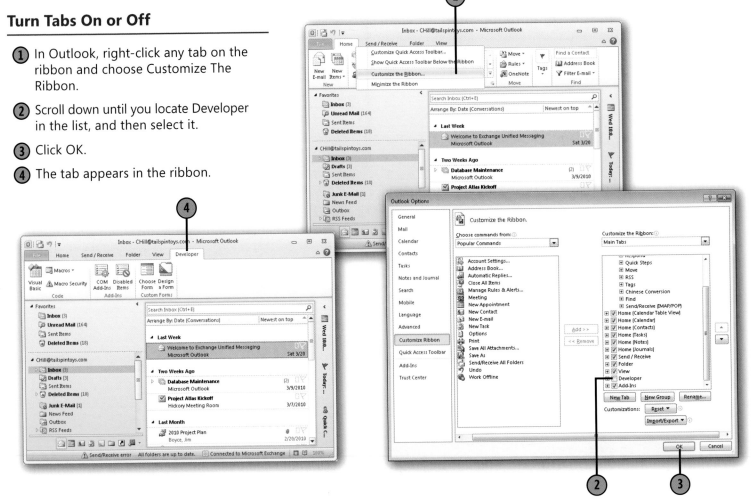

Add Your Own Tab

1 Right-click any tab on the ribbon and choose Customize The Ribbon.

2 Click New Tab.

3 A New Tab item appears in the list.

4 Click on the newly created tab.

5 Click Rename.

6 Type a new name.

7 Click OK.

(continued on next page)

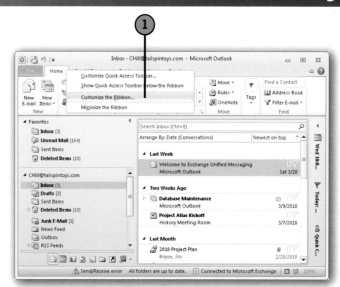

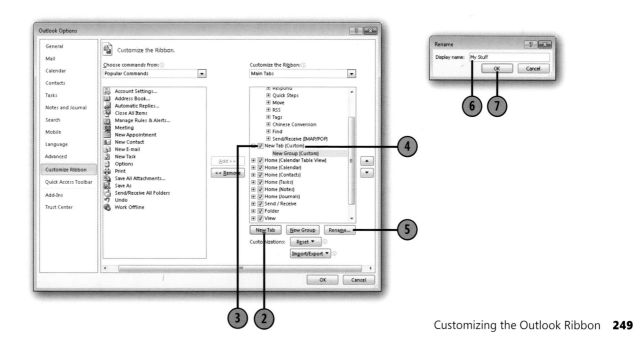

Add Your Own Tab *(continued)*

8 Click New Group (Custom), which is created by default when you add the tab.

9 Click Rename.

10 Type a name for the group.

11 Choose an icon for the group.

12 Click OK.

13 Choose a command group from the drop-down list.

14 Choose a command.

15 Click the Add button to add the command to the selected group.

16 Add other commands and groups as you want and click OK.

17 The new items appear in your custom tab. (This example shows two new groups.)

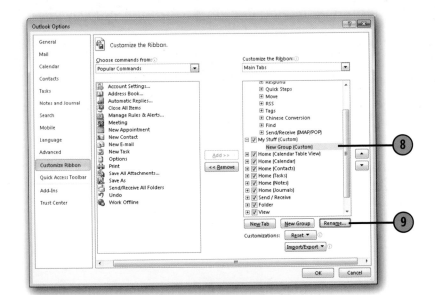

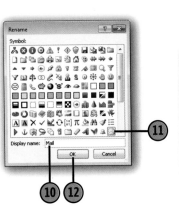

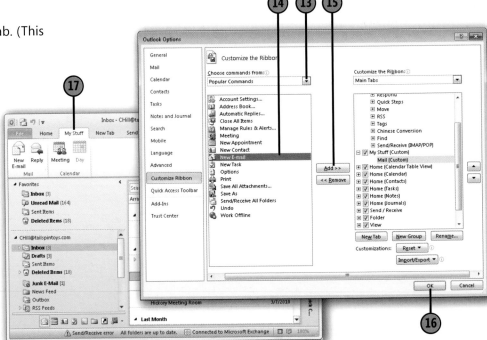

Customizing the Quick Access Toolbar

The Quick Access Toolbar by default sits above the ribbon and provides quick access (hence its name) to frequently used commands and options. The Quick Access Toolbar takes up relatively little space, so it's unobtrusive. Although it already contains a handful of commands, you can add your own to suit your needs.

1. Click the Customize Quick Access Toolbar button.

2. Choose More Commands.

3. Choose a command group.

4. Choose the command you want to add.

5. Click Add.

6. Add any other commands as you like, and click OK.

7. The commands now appear in the Quick Access Toolbar.

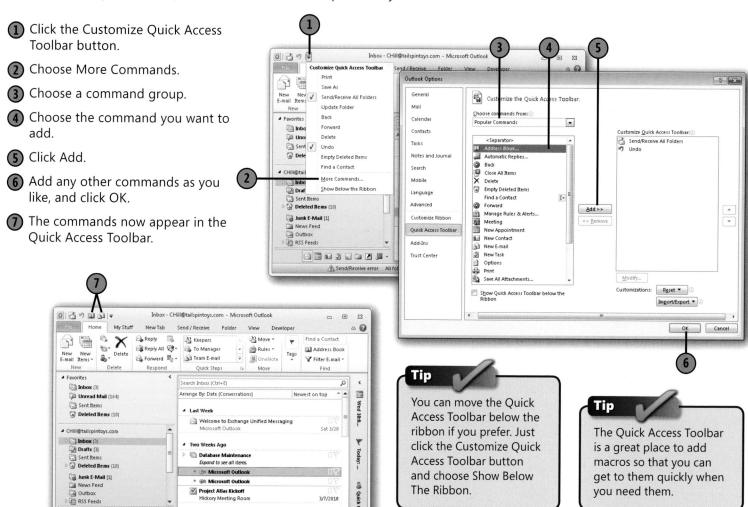

Tip

You can move the Quick Access Toolbar below the ribbon if you prefer. Just click the Customize Quick Access Toolbar button and choose Show Below The Ribbon.

Tip

The Quick Access Toolbar is a great place to add macros so that you can get to them quickly when you need them.

Index

Symbols

R

reading e-mail, 74–75
Reading Pane, 34
    RSS feed preview in, 93
    sender's online availability display in, 200
    turning off, 75
reading RSS feed article online, 98
read receipts for e-mail messages, 238
Really Simple Syndication (RSS). *See* RSS feeds
receiving e-mail, 72–73
recovering deleted messages, 76
recovery from backups, testing, 234
recurring appointments, 137
recurring meetings, 123, 125
recurring tasks, 156–157
"RE:" in subject line, 81
reminders, 144
    for meetings, 123
    for tasks, 150
    setting up for mobile devices, 184
    sound for, 155
removing. *See* deleting
reply to e-mail, 81
Request A Delivery Receipt option, 238
Request A Read Receipt option, 238
resizing. *See* sizing
resources, scheduling use, 134
retention policies, administrator settings for, 233
reversing sort order of messages, 74
ribbon, 30. *See also* names of individual tabs
    adding tab, 249–250
    new features, 6–7
    turning on or off, 248

Rich Site Summary. *See* RSS feeds
Rich Text, for e-mail message, 239
Rich Text Format
    and HTML stationery, 62
    for e-mail message, 57
RSS Feed dialog box, 92
RSS feeds, 91
    adding automatically, 92
    downloading full article, 98
    folder name changes, 94
    folders for
        changing, 95
    for calendar updates, 189
    message management, 96–98
    viewing, 93
Rules Wizard, 86–88
    creating rule based on message, 86
    creating rule from scratch, 87–88

S

saving
    attachments to e-mail, 80
    e-mail messages, 77
Scheduling Assistant, 134, 136
Search Folder Criteria dialog box, 212
search folders, 211–214
    creating custom, 212–213
    modifying, 214
searching
    for activities associated with contact, 109
    for contacts, 112–114
    for older messages during cleanup, 219
Search tab in ribbon, 24–25
Search Tools in ribbon, 114
selected tasks, printing list, 169
Select Members dialog box, 52
Select Names dialog box, 48, 55

sender
    removing from Junk Mail list, 85
    sorting e-mail by, 74
sending
    e-mail messages, 66–67
    invitation to meeting, 20
    text message, 28
sending text messages from Outlook, 182
Send/Receive tab in ribbon
    Send/Receive All Folders, 73
    Send/Receive Groups, 73
Sent messages, reviewing, 68
server alerts to mobile device, 26
Setup Wizard, 2
SharePoint
    adding calendars to Outlook, 188–192
        connecting SharePoint 2007 calendar, 190
        connecting SharePoint 2010 calendar, 188–189
    contacts use in Outlook, 193–195
    creating calendar items in Outlook, 191–192
    creating contact from Outlook, 194–195
    document libraries use in Outlook, 196–197
    Outlook Social Connector, 198
SharePoint Lists, 8
SharePoint Workspace, 197
sharing contact group, 52
sharing information
    for tasks, 169
    from Calendar, 145–146
shortcut for Outlook, 32
shortcuts
    creating for folder, 244–245
    dragging items to create, 246
    for non-Outlook items, 247
    for Web sites, 245

V

W

About the Author

Jim Boyce has authored or coauthored more than 45 books about computer hardware and software, including *Microsoft® Office® Outlook 2007 Plain & Simple* and *Microsoft® Outlook® Version 2002 Inside Out*. He is a former contributing editor and monthly columnist for *WINDOWS Magazine*. He has worked with computers as a programmer and systems manager in a variety of capacities since the 1970s, and has a wide range of experience in the MS-DOS, Microsoft Windows, Microsoft Windows NT, and UNIX environments.

What do you think of this book?

We want to hear from you!

To participate in a brief online survey, please visit:

microsoft.com/learning/booksurvey

Tell us how well this book meets your needs—what works effectively, and what we can do better. Your feedback will help us continually improve our books and learning resources for you.

Thank you in advance for your input!

Stay in touch!

To subscribe to the *Microsoft Press® Book Connection Newsletter*—for news on upcoming books, events, and special offers—please visit:

microsoft.com/learning/books/newsletter